Essential
Athens

by Mike Gerrard

*Above: the Parthenon, crowning glory of the
Acropolis of Athens*

PASSPORT BOOKS
NTC/Contemporary Publishing Group

Traditional folk costumes are saved for special occasions, such as Independence Day

Front cover: *the Parthenon; traditional Greek costume; worry . beads*
Front cover: *sun-dried tomatoes*

Published by Passport Books, a division of NTC/Contemporary Publishing Group, Inc. 4255 West Touhy Avenue, Lincolnwood (Chicago), Illinois 60646-1975, U.S.A.

Copyright © The Automobile Association 1999
Maps © The Automobile Association 1999

The Automobile Association retains the copyright in the original edition © 1999 and in all subsequent editions, reprints, and amendments.

The contents of this publication are believed correct at the time of printing. Nevertheless, the publishers cannot accept responsibility for errors or omissions, or for changes in details given. We are always grateful to readers who let us know of any errors or omissions they come across, and future printings will be updated accordingly.

Published by Passport Books in conjunction with The Automobile Association of Great Britain.

Written by Mike Gerrard

Library of Congress Catalog Card Number: 98-68313
ISBN 0-8442-2210-0

Color separation: Pace Colour, Southampton

Printed and bound in Italy by Printer Trento srl

Contents

About this Book

KEY TO SYMBOLS

🚩 map reference to the maps in the What to See section

✉ address

☎ telephone number

🕐 opening times

🍽 restaurant or café on premises or near by

🚇 nearest underground train station

🚌 nearest bus/tram route

🚉 nearest overground train station

🛥 nearest ferry stop

♿ facilities for visitors with disablilities

✋ admission charge

↔ other places of interest near by

❓ other practical information

Essential *Athens* is divided into five sections to cover the most important aspects of your visit to Athens.

Viewing Athens pages 5–14
An introduction to Athens by the author
    Athens's Features
    Essence of Athens
    The Shaping of Athens
    Peace and Quiet
    Athens's Famous

Top Ten pages 15–26
The author's choice of the Top Ten places to see in Athens, listed in alphabetical order, each with practical information.

What to See pages 27–90
The city of Athens and excursions from the city, each with its own brief introduction and an alphabetical listing of the main attractions
    Practical information
    Snippets of 'Did you know…' information
    5 suggested walks
    3 suggested tours
    2 features

Where To... pages 91–116
Detailed listings of the best places to eat, stay, shop, take the children and be entertained.

Practical Matters pages 117–24
A highly visual section containing essential travel information.

Maps
All map references are to the individual maps found in the What to See section of this guide.
For example, the Acropolis has the reference 🚩 28C2 – indicating the page on which the map is located and the grid square in which the Acropolis is to be found. A list of the maps that have been used in this travel guide can be found in the index.

Greek Placenames
Romanised spellings of Greek names can vary. In placename headings and in the index, this book uses transliterations which follow a recognised convention and which correspond to AA maps. More familiar Anglicised spellings (given in brackets in the headings) are sometimes used in the text.

Prices
Where appropriate, an indication of the cost of an establishment is given by **£** signs: **£££** denotes higher prices, **££** denotes average prices, while **£** denotes lower charges.

Star Ratings
Most of the places described in this book have been given a separate rating:
✪✪✪   Do not miss
✪✪   Highly recommended
✪   Worth seeing

Viewing
Athens

Above: *the Temple of Hephaistos in the Agora*
Right: *this female figure from the Goulandris Museum of Cycladic Art is at least 4000 years old*

Mike Gerrard's Athens

Safe and Cheap
Athens is the cheapest capital city in Europe, according to figures produced by Eurostat, the official European Union statistical publication. And Greece is the second safest country in Europe for tourists, according to French research based on theft per 1,000 residents. Portugal is safest with only two reports, then Greece with four, compared to 27 in Britain and 37 in Holland.

Each time I visit Greece's capital, I seem to see one incident which captures the city for me. For the previous edition of this book, it was a scooter rider driving through a 'No Entry' sign and then along the pavement among the pedestrians, since that was the quickest way to his destination. Obey the one-way system? Not the Greeks. While researching this new edition, it was again a scooter rider. This young man raced through a busy city crossroads and, while turning right, took one hand off the handlebars and crossed himself three times because he was passing a church. Only in Athens, I thought.

Many visitors to Athens just see the traffic, and not the people. Athens is indeed far too busy and noisy, and bedevilled with smog, and too hot in August. And yet, and yet... the city is making great efforts to improve the centre. There are constant schemes to restrict traffic access. One of the main shopping streets, Ermou, has been pedestrianised for much of its length, making it a pleasant place to stroll along in the day, and again at night when the buskers emerge. There is talk of more pedestrianisation, and of creating a traffic-free triangle based around Ermou. Monuments like the Acropolis stand aloof from the traffic. Byzantine churches ignore the hubbub. The National Archaeological Museum remains one of the finest museums in the world. And the Athenians remain resolutely themselves, at home in their city, as any visitor could be if he or she remembers to look for the little human touches.

Scooters are an ever-present feature of Athens

Athens's Features

Wet or Dry
• It rains in Athens for about 100 days each year. However, all that rain only amounts to 400mm per annum, falling mainly in the winter and hardly at all from July to September. July and August are equally hot, with an average temperature of 32°C. The coldest month is January, averaging 12°C.

Population
• Almost four million people live in the Greater Athens area. This is nearly a quarter of the Greek population. In the late 19th century, the population was only 124,000.

Area
• The Greater Athens area covers 427sq km, and is mostly surrounded by natural boundaries. The Aegean Sea is to the south, while to the northeast, northwest, east and west are the hill and mountain ranges of Pentelikon, Parnes, Hymettus and Aegaleos respectively. The highest of these is the Parnes range, rising to 1,413m.

Small Firms
• In Greater Athens there are roughly 50,000 small industrial companies, although the vast majority actually employ five persons or fewer.

Initially Athens
• Visitors will regularly see certain sets of initials in Athens, among them the following:
EHS The urban railway service
ELPA The Touring and Automobile Club of Greece
ELTA The Post Office
EOT Tourist information offices (NTOG overseas)
KTEL The private bus service
OASA/ETHEL The public bus service
OSE The Railway Organisation
OTE The telephone service

No Problem?
Greeks smoke eight cigarettes per person per day – twice as many as in England and three times as many as in Sweden. A recent survey showed that only 9 per cent of Greeks said that they were very satisfied with their life, compared with 28 per cent of English people. Perhaps the worry beads don't work after all!

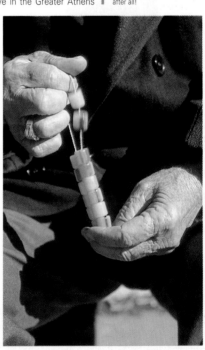

Worry beads can still be seen – and heard – in the cáfes of Athens, and bought as souvenirs

Essence of Athens

Arriving in Athens and seeing the Acropolis standing proud above the city cannot fail to lift the spirits, for the first-time and return visitor alike. Athens is an ancient city with many layers of history, most of them on show in the National Archaeological Museum, but it is also a modern city where history is still very much in the making: the rule of the Colonels, more recent political scandals, the forthcoming Olympic Games. All these are part of the fabric of life here, and your visit will be all the richer if you consider the present as well as the past. But what a past it has!

Right: a splendid Guardsman Below: sunrise over Athens - the Theatre of Herodes Atticus

THE 10 ESSENTIALS

If you only have a short time to visit Athens, or would like to get a really complete picture of the city, here are the essentials:

• **Visit the Acropolis** (► 17), one of the world's greatest buildings. To beat the crowds, be the first one there when it opens.

• **See the National Archaeological Museum** (► 18), allowing at least a half-day to appreciate its many treasures.

• **Stroll the Pláka** at night (► 25), when the locals and tourists throng the mostly traffic-free streets, enjoying the atmosphere and a good evening meal.

• **See the Sunday morning flea market** around Monastiráki (► 50), all bustle and bargains, and the kind of place about which they say, 'if you can't buy it here then it can't be bought'.

• **Eat in a busy taverna.** My own favourite is the Sigalas (► 95) on Monastiráki Square, especially for a weekend lunch.

• **Eat in a good restaurant.** Splash out on a meal at one of the many fine eating places in Athens (► 92–9). You don't have to stick to *souvlaki* and Greek salad.

• **Drink retsina.** It's an acquired taste, and you may not acquire it, but you should always try the local drink, if only once.

• **Enter a church** to see the icons and sit a while, watching Athenians come and go. It's also an escape from the noise and traffic.

• **Linger over a coffee or an ouzo.** Have a coffee in the daytime or a pre-dinner ouzo, while watching the Athenian world go by.

• **See some of the lesser-known museums**: the Goulandris Museum of Cycladic Art (► 24) is stunning, the Museum of Greek Musical Instruments (► 23) terrific fun, and many of the smaller museums, like the Kanellopoulos Museum (► 53), contain items of exquisite beauty.

Above: *eating in Athens is a family occasion, and often enjoyed outdoors*
Inset: *if a waiter can't tempt you to eat, he will still gladly give the visitor directions*

The Shaping of Athens

*c*3000 BC
Evidence of first settlements around the Acropolis.

1400
The Acropolis becomes a royal fortress.

800–600
The first city-states emerge, including Athens. Kings are replaced by annually appointed 'archons' from leading families.

620
Draco formalises the laws of Athens and Attica; their strictness gives us the word 'draconian'.

594–3
Athens receives a new Constitution, created by the politician Solon. A 'Council of 400' is established, heralding the birth of democracy.

520–430
The Persian Wars.

490
The Battle of Marathon and the defeat of the invading Persians by the Athenians.

480
The Persians, led by Xerxes, gain their revenge at Thermopylae and take Athens, but the Athenians then win the Battle of Salamis.

479
The Persians are finally defeated.

461–429
The Golden Age of Pericles, the building of the Parthenon, the era of Sophocles, Aeschylus and Euripides.

429
Death of Pericles.

431–404
The Peloponnesian Wars result in the defeat of Athens by Sparta.

371
Sparta in its turn is defeated by Thebes.

338
Philip II of Macedon conquers and rules Greece.

336
The murder of Philip II and the succession of his son, Alexander the Great.

336–23
The age of Alexander the Great, who extends his empire throughout the Middle East, and the Mediterranean, reaching as far as India.

A coin depicting Alexander the Great, wearing a ram's horns as a sign of his divinity

323
The death of Alexander the Great.

200 BC–AD 300
The Romans conquer and rule Greece, creating many of the city's fine monuments.

AD 50
The Apostle Paul visits Athens to preach.

324
Emperor Constantine establishes Constantinople (formerly Byzantium) as the capital of the eastern part of the Roman Empire.

1204
Franks and Venetians take Constantinople and divide Greece between them.

1261–2
The Byzantine Empire re-takes Constantinople and much of mainland Greece.

1429
The Turks capture Thessaloniki.

1453
The fall of Constantinople (Istanbul) and the end of the Byzantine Empire.

1453–1821
Greece comes under Ottoman rule.

1821–9
The Greek War of Independence.

1832
Prince Otto of Bavaria elected the first king of the modern Greek state.

1917
Greece enters World War I on the side of the Allies.

1920–3
Greece continues a misjudged war against Turkey, ending in inevitable defeat.

1923
The exchange of populations, when over one million Greeks in Turkey return to their homeland, while 400,000 Muslims leave Greece for Turkey. Many of the immigrants settle in Piraeus.

Colonel Papadopoulos, the new Greek Prime Minister, addresses the local and world press

1940
Mussolini demands access to Greek ports in World War II. The Greek General Metaxas gives a one-word answer, 'Óchi' (No).

1941
The Italian and German invasions lead to desperate food shortages in Athens, where an estimated 40,000 people die.

1944
Greece is liberated. Churchill visits Athens to show his support.

1951
Greece joins NATO.

1952
Greek women receive the vote.

1967
A military junta seizes power and King Constantine flees into exile. Rule of the Colonels, under Colonel Papadopoulos.

1974
The junta is overthrown in Athens and democracy returns.

1975
A new republican constitution means the final abandonment of the monarchy.

1981
Greece joins the European Community and Athens becomes a European capital.

1985
Athens becomes Europe's first Cultural Capital, an idea devised by the Greek politician and former actress, Melina Mercouri.

2004
Athens is to host the Olympic Games.

Peace & Quiet

Athens is a city where you will almost certainly want peace and quiet at some stage of your visit, as it cannot be denied that it is a noisy metropolis. Yet, even if Athens is not the greenest city in the world, there are places to go to escape the traffic and its attendant pollution.

Ethnikós Kípos (National Gardens)

Below: *the walk down from Lykabettos Hill is much easier than the hike to the top*
Inset: *the colourful Cretzschmar's bunting*

These pleasant gardens (► 37) present one refuge, with their shady walks and plenty of benches on which to sit and read a paper. You might also be able to enjoy the sound of songbirds in the spring. The best time to see birds is from approximately March till late June, when the city's nesting residents are joined by migrating species such as swifts. The birds are most active in the early mornings and again in the evenings when the heat of the afternoon has gone.

Lykavittós (Lykabettos Hill)

Meander along the pathways to the top of Lykabettos Hill (► 21) – or if tired take the funicular up and walk down – and you may come across nightingales, shrikes, warblers and the stunning, but shy, golden orioles. Look out for the lizards and butterflies too.

Kerameikós Cemetery and the Agorá

Many of the archaeological sites also provide refuge both for wildlife and for the tired visitor. The Kerameikós Cemetery (► 45) is a haven for lizards, tortoises and a variety of bird life, such as redstarts, nuthatches and the blue rock thrushes. It can also be peaceful to sit in the quieter parts of the large Agorá (► 16), as most visitors speedily see the main highlights and leave again without venturing to the further reaches.

Greek Islands

If it's real peace you seek, and not merely a temporary reprieve from the city, take the metro to Piraeus and remember that the closest Greek islands are less than an hour away. You may be lucky enough to spot dolphins swimming alongside the ferries, or see flying fishes leaping out of the water, both of which are reasonably common occurrences in the Aegean.

Graceful monuments in the tranquil setting of the Kerameikós Cemetery

Rámnoús and Brauron

Athens does have an urban sprawl, but it is much more compact than most other European capitals. Greece is a rural country and nearby sites such as Rámnoús (► 88) and Vavróna (Brauron ► 90) offer an incredible contrast to the pace of city life. Take a picnic to Rámnoús and your only company is likely to be the site attendant, along with birds, butterflies, crickets and lizards.

Delphi

More spectacular wildlife can be seen on the easy-to-arrange day-trips to places such as Delfoí (Delphi ► 78) and Epídavros (► 80). Delphi is particularly likely to produce some impressive birds of prey, despite its constant stream of visitors. Climb up above the theatre to the stadium beneath the slopes of the Parnassos Mountains and you will escape many of the crowds. If you can time your visit for the moment the gates are opened, or for the end of the day, you stand much more chance, not just of peace and quiet, but of seeing local raptors such as vultures, falcons and even golden eagles. Look out, too, for the many orchids which grow here, despite this being one of Greece's most visited sites.

Athens's Famous

Melina Mercouri was equally successful as actress and politician

Melina Mercouri

Like Ronald Reagan, Melina Mercouri was an actor turned politician. Born in Athens in 1922, she achieved great fame on both stage and film, initially in Greece but then worldwide, with starring roles in films such as *Never on Sunday* and *Topkapi*. When she turned to politics she proved to be both an extremely able and extremely popular politician. She never lost her sense of the theatrical, a quality the Greeks admire, and she became the country's Minister of Culture in 1981. She suggested the idea of highlighting a different capital city each year as the European City of Culture, an idea which has transformed many cities. Athens was the first to be chosen, in 1985. Mercouri also mounted a continuing campaign to retrieve the Elgin Marbles from the British Museum and return them to Athens. She died in 1994 and is buried in the First Cemetery.

The Elgin Marbles

Pericles hired the renowned sculptor Pheidias to oversee the work on the Parthenon, including the building's remarkable friezes. In 1801 the Acropolis buildings were in ruins, neglected by the Ottoman rulers. The British Lord Elgin negotiated permission to remove some of the ancient remains. In fact, he removed more than he should have. He then sold what are now called the Elgin Marbles to the British Museum, who have resisted all Greek pleas to return them.

Lord Byron

The British poet Lord Byron (1788–1824) is a revered figure in Greece, and many places have streets named in his honour (Vyronos). He was a high-profile campaigner in the Greek War of Independence, and was prepared to fight, but instead died of a fever in Missolonghi. He first visited Athens in 1809 when he was 21, and was inspired to write two works that helped make him famous: 'Maid of Athens' and *Childe Harold's Pilgrimage*.

Pericles

Pericles was born in about 495 BC and became the greatest statesman in Athenian history. He was a visionary, with an interest in the arts and sciences, who transformed the look of the city to such an extent that the period between 461 and 429 BC became known as the Golden Age of Pericles. By 461 BC he had become the leader of a democratic party, and by 443 BC he was both ruler and military leader of Athens. Having transferred the Treasury to Athens from Delos, he persuaded the Athenians to invest in a programme of building and rebuilding, which brought together the best contemporary architects, sculptors, artists, scientists and builders. The

results can still be seen today. Most notable are the buildings on top of the Acropolis, with the Parthenon representing Pericles's outstanding legacy. Pericles was also an adept military leader, combining bravery and diplomacy. He died in 429 BC after contracting the plague that swept through the Athens he had done so much to beautify.

Pericles, the man who changed the face of Athens

Top Ten

Above: *the Stoa of Attalos in the Agora*
Right: *one of the many fine statues contained in the Agora Museum*

1
Agorá

The Agora, once home to market, mint, prison, theatres and schools

After the Acropolis, the market place of ancient Athens is the other 'must see'. It features some good remains and a fine, small museum.

✚ 28B2

✉ Adrianou 24

☎ 321-0185

🕐 Tue–Sun 8:30–2:45. Closed public holidays

🍴 None

🚇 Theseion/Monastiráki

♿ None

✋ Expensive; free Sun

↔ Monastiráki (► 50), Acropolis (► 17), Pláka (► 25)

Imagine the Agorá (Agora) filled with stalls and shops, its streets and squares packed with buyers and sellers. It helps to buy a plan or to consult one of the information boards dotted around the site. The area was first used as a market place in about the 6th century BC; before that it was a cemetery. The site was at the heart of Athenian life for centuries, along with the Acropolis, which rises behind it. In fact, a good overview of the Agora can be had from the Acropolis, or from the neighbouring Areopagos (► 35).

At ground level the foundations of many buildings are still evident, with signs in English for some of them. Two buildings dominate opposite ends of the site. One is the Temple of Hephaistos (► 39), and the other the Stoa Atallou (Stoa of Attalos), which contains the Agora's excellent little museum. The Stoa is a two-storey arcade, first built in the 2nd century BC, which has been immaculately restored by the American School of Archaeology in Athens, giving us a rare opportunity to see what Greek buildings of the period actually looked like. Inside, the museum is full of quirky finds that bring old Athens to life: a child's commode, a fragment of a library rule-book, a machine used for the selection of officials. Between the museum and the Acropolis is another restored building, the Church of the Holy Apostles (► 32).

2
Akrópoli (Acropolis)

Acropolis means 'upper city', and refers to the outcrop of rock that rises above the city around which Athens was founded and later flourished.

The Acrópolis of Athens is as striking by night as by day

There are several buildings on top of the Acropolis. All were part of a building boom instigated by Pericles (➤ 14) in the 5th century BC. The finest of these is the Parthenon. The city's greatest sculptors worked on the building, achieving a consistently pleasing whole under the guidance of the greatest sculptor of them all, Pheidias. Despite the apparent geometrical symmetry, there are no straight lines in the Parthenon's construction, as all its floors, columns and friezes taper very subtly to create a visual harmony. It is built of a marble which contains some iron, and this contributes to the stunning golden glow that the building develops in a good sunset. It is also a thrilling sight at night, when it is illuminated.

Several other buildings make up the Acropolis, including the Propylaia, which is on the left as you enter and was the original imposing gateway. The small Temple of Athena Nike (Athena, Bringer of Victory) was demolished by the Turks in 1686, but lovingly restored in the 19th century. The Eréchtheio, on the far side of the Sacred Way from the Parthenon, is said to have been the place where Athena brought forth the first olive tree. An impressive collection of finds is in the Museum, though some of the best of these are slowly being transferred to the more impressive Acropolis Study Centre (➤ 20).

✚ 28C2

☎ Site 321-0219, museum 323-6665

🕑 Site Mon–Fri 8–6:30, Sat–Sun 8–2:30; museum Mon 10:30–6:30, Tue–Sun 8–2:30. Closed public holidays

🍽 None

🚇 Monastiráki/Theiseion

♿ None

💰 Expensive (combined entrance ticket to site and museum); free Sun

↔ Agorá(➤ 16), Pnyka(➤ 63), Acropolis Study Centre (➤ 18)

❓ Sound and light show, seating and tickets on the Pnyka

3

Ethnikó Archaiologikó Mouseío (National Archeological Museum

Poseidon, one of the elder trinity of the Greek gods

This is one of the world's great museums, ranking alongside the British Museum in London and the Louvre in Paris.

You should allow at least half a day, or two visits, if you hope to explore fully the largest collection of Greek art in the world. Highlights include the beautiful frescoes from houses on Thíra (Santorini), which were contemporaneous with the Cretan Minoan civilisation before being engulfed in the island's massive earthquake. Elsewhere are the treasures from Mycenae, including the gold mask which caused archaeologist Heinrich Schliemann to declare, 'I have gazed upon the face of Agamemnon'. More recent experts have thrown great doubt upon Schliemann's impulsive and bold claim. Many of the statues in the museum will be familiar, including a magnificent figure of a powerful Poseidon about to throw his trident, while on a more delicate scale the 'Jockey-boy' of Artemission shows a young boy encouraging his horse with great urgency and grace.

If time is limited, then the following 'highlights' tour may help. On going through the doors to the left of the main entrance hall, walk straight ahead as far as you can go, turn right, and a few rooms ahead of you is the imposing statue of Poseidon. At the far end of that gallery, turn right and walk to the marbled central hall where the 'Jockey-boy' bronze statue is displayed. Both this and the statue of Poseidon were found together, in 1927, in the seas off the island of Evia. The stairs to the upper floor are now on your left. In the room to the left at the foot of the stairs is a marvellous collection of bronzes, including a rampant satyr, familiar

✚ 28C5

✉ Oktovnou 28–Patission 44

☎ 821-7717

🕐 Mon 12:30–6:45, Tue–Fri 8–6:45 (closes at 3PM in winter), Sat–Sun 8:30–2:45. Closed public holidays. Gift shop Tue–Sat 8:30–2:30

🍴 Café (££)

Ⓜ Omonia

♿ None

✋ Expensive; free Sun

↔ Exárchia (➤ 38)

❓ Guided tours available in several languages

from risqué Greek postcards, yet so tiny in actuality that many visitors pass by without noticing it. At the top of the stairs, straight ahead up a few more steps, is the collection of delicate frescoes from Santorini, dating from about 1500 BC. Note the two young boys boxing, and wall paintings of monkeys, flowers and antelopes. On walking back down the stairs you will find the temporary exhibition halls to your left; these often stage some remarkable exhibitions. If, however, you walk straight ahead you will come to the Mycenean Hall, containing the great golden treasures from that ancient palace complex. As well as the renowned death masks (at 1500 BC contemporaneous with the Thíra frescoes), make sure you also see the bull's head with its golden horns, a breathtakingly beautiful creation.

Below: *the museum is set in a small but pleasant park*
Inset: *vases from the island of Santorini, whose frescoes on the upper floors are a star attraction*

If you would like to know more about the collection, guides can be hired for personal tours in English, French, German, Italian and Spanish; you can ask for short or long tours. Booking is at the entrance next to the stairs leading to the basement café, where you will also find a display of casts and reproductions from the collection for sale. This is closed on Sundays.

A separate coin collection in the Numismatic Museum, displaying only some of its 400,000 coins, is accessible on the first floor or from a side entrance at Tositsa 1, though the collection has been closed for some time awaiting its removal to Schliemann's House (▶ 67).

4
Kéntro Meletón Akropóleos
(Acropolis Study Centre)

Light and spacious, the new Acropolis Study Centre is expanding year by year

The centre is an enterprising project, designed to illustrate all aspects of the building and history of the Acropolis.

✝ 28C1

✉ Makriyianni 2–4

☎ 923-9381

🕐 Daily 9–2:30. Closed public holidays

🚌 230

♿ None

✋ Free

↔ Acropolis (➤ 17), Theatre of Dionysos (➤ 68), Odeon of Herodes Atticus (➤ 54), Ilias Lalaounis Jewellery Museum (➤ 54)

This ancient Athenian waits in the entrance to the centre

A building site still surrounds the first main structure to be completed – a converted army barracks. The original idea behind the centre was supported by Melina Mercouri, the Greek Minister of Culture, with the hope that one day the Elgin Marbles (➤ 14) would be returned to Athens from the British Museum in London and put on display here. For the moment, the centre contains replicas of the main friezes from the Parthenon. Their scale is wonderfully impressive in these surroundings as you are much closer to them than is possible at the Parthenon itself. The skill of the workmen, the subtlety of their carvings and the imposing design all become plainly evident, and anyone who visits the Acropolis should certainly visit the Study Centre as well.

Other displays explain how the Acropolis was built, and how the marble for the buildings was quarried and brought to Athens from the surrounding hills. You can see how the carvings were made, how the columns were then erected, the changing face of the Acropolis, the building tools used, and the preservation and restoration work that has been undertaken. An architect's model of the centre is on show, along with the other designs submitted. The small part of the complex that has been completed is impressive enough, so a view of the finished centre makes the visitor more sympathetic to the bulldozers and dust outside.

5
Lykavittós
(Lykabettos Hill)

The highest hill in Athens at 278m, Lykabettos dominates the city almost as much as the Acropolis, of which there is an excellent view from the top.

Lykabettos was once well outside the city boundaries, because, as recently as the 19th century, Athens was merely a small cluster of houses around the Acropolis. It is hard to imagine that today, as you gaze out from the hilltop and see the modern metropolis sprawling before you, all the way to Piraeus on the coast. Some of the offshore islands in the Saronic Gulf can also be seen, including Salamis (► 88) and, on a clear day, even Aegina (► 75).

To the north is Mount Parnes. It's a stiff climb to get to the top of this chalk outcrop, but a very pleasant one – through pine-scented woods, often filled with butterflies, and even a few wild tortoises (► 12–13). There are several routes up, plenty of benches on which to take a breather, a café half-way up and another at the very top. Here, too, is the small, whitewashed 19th-century chapel of Ágios Geórgios (St George), whose feast is celebrated on 23 April. Below the summit, on the far side, is the modern, open-air Lykabettos Theatre, where concerts are frequently held: dance, jazz, classical and rock. It is also possible to take a funicular to the top and back; this stays open till 10PM reflecting the popularity of the hill at night. This is the perfect place for a late-night coffee or brandy, with the illuminated city spread out at your feet.

🕇 29E4

🚡 Funicular from the corner of Aristippou and Ploutarchou daily 8AM–10PM

🍴 Cafés (£££)

🚌 023

♿ None

✋ Free open access

↔ Kolonáki (► 46)

Pine woods cloak the slopes of Lykavittós, once home to wolves (lykoi)

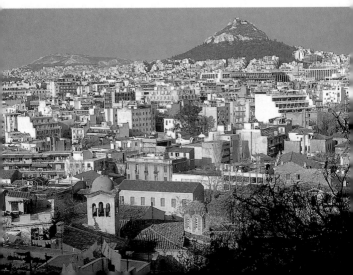

6
Mouseío Ellinikís Laografias (Museum of Greek Folk Art)

The Museum of Greek Folk Art has an excellent collection, which gives a fascinating insight into Greek folk traditions.

Greece preserves its folk traditions well, both in everyday life and in museums such as this one, in the Pláka district. On the ground floor are embroidery displays from the different island groups and also from the mainland. Ali Pasha's court at Ioannina exerted a strong influence on local embroidery, importing rich fabrics from the Near East and from as far away as Iran and Uzbekistan.

✚ 57C1

✉ Kydathinaion 17

☎ 321-3018, 322-9031

🕐 Tue–Sun 10–2. Closed public holidays

🚌 024, 230

♿ Few

✋ Moderate

↔ Acropolis (▶ 17), Anafiótika (▶ 83), Hellenic Children's Museum (▶ 36), Museum of Greek Children's Art (▶ 52), Pláka (▶ 25)

❓ Special exhibitions

Rich traditional costumes showing expert embroidery skills

The Mezzanine displays some ornate spinning wheels, shuttles and spindles, together with examples of work, such as a pillowcase woven by nomadic Sarakatsan shepherds. There are some bread seals, for both family and religious occasions (though frequently in Greece, the one is the other), including one that imprints on the loaf 'The one who eats of my body and drinks of my blood'. There are also several masquerade costumes, the most famous of which is probably the Skyros Goat Dancer, the Yeros, with his masked face, sheepskin coat and dangling bells. A permanent display on the same floor is dedicated to the folk artist Theofilos Hatzimichael (c1868–1934). Especially worth seeing is the Theofilos room, dating from 1924–30, from a house on Lesvos, where every inch of wall space is covered in primitive but vibrant paintings, including Alexander the Great, folk hero Katsantonis and political hero Kolokotronis. Silverware includes earrings and necklaces, belts and buckles, and religious objects such as a Bible, printed in Venice in 1754, but with a Greek-made silver binding showing the Resurrection.

On the ground floor is a small shop selling some craft items and a good selection of books.

7

Mouseío Ellinikón Mousikon Orgánon (Museum of Greek Musical Instruments)

This specialist museum in a handsome Pláka mansion is a must, whether you have a passion for, or merely a passing interest in, Greek music.

The mansion was built in 1842, and outside is a pleasant courtyard in which occasional concerts are held in the summer. Off the courtyard is the museum's shop, with an extensive collection of recordings and books on Greek music for sale. The interior of the mansion has been renovated to create three floors of display space devoted to the subject of Greek musical instruments. This is only part of the collection of over 1,200 instruments, dating back to the 18th century, amassed by musicologist Fivos Anoyanakis.

Inside the entrance is a small video display area showing films covering the making and playing of different instruments. The fun starts with the display cases themselves, however, as most of them have headphones attached, enabling you to listen to the instruments being played. A brief introduction in Greek and then English tells you which instrument in the case you are listening to, the name of the tune and where it was recorded. To listen to all the recordings available would take hours, and it is not unusual to see people not merely tapping their feet but dancing to the music! The instruments are grouped according to type and many of them are exquisite works of craftsmanship. Take a look at some of the lyres and guitars, in particular. On a simpler level, one set of photographs shows you how to make music using worry beads and a wine glass! There are also rural instruments such as bagpipes and shepherd's pipes, and examples of the urban blues known as *rembetika*.

✚	57C2
✉	Diogenous 1–3
☎	325-0198/4119
🕑	Tue, Thu–Sun 10–2, Wed 12–6. Closed public holidays
🍴	None
Ⓜ	Monastiráki
♿	None
✋	Free
↔	Acropolis (➤ 17), Kanellopoulos Museum (➤ 53), Pláka (➤ 25), Roman Agora (➤ 67), Tower of the Winds (➤ 54)
❓	Summer concerts: call museum for details

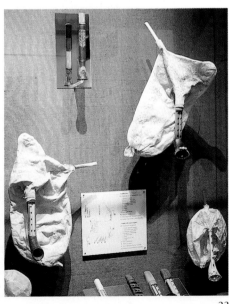

Bagpipes such as these are often made from the stomachs of animals

8
Mouseío Kykladikís kai Archaías Ellinikí Téchnis (Museum of Cycladic Art)

✝ 29E3

✉ Neofytou Douka 4

☎ 722-8321, 724-9706 (shop)

🕐 Mon, Wed–Fri 10–4; Sat 10–3. Closed Tue, Sun, public holidays

🍴 Café (££)

🚌 234

♿ None

✋ Cheap

↔ Benaki Museum (➤ 51), Byzantine Museum (➤ 69), War Museum (➤ 64), Kolonáki (➤ 46)

The museum houses items that date back some 5,000 years

This first-class modern museum houses the remarkable private collection of Nikolas P Goulandris, a shipowner and patron of the arts.

The displays span many centuries of ancient Greek art – vases, glassware and other items – but the central exhibits are the beautiful artifacts from the Cycladic civilisation of 3000–2000 BC. The statues are especially memorable – the figures seem to float in their display cabinets as subtle lighting brings out their shape and texture. It will be a rare visitor who is not tempted to take home a copy from the attractive museum shop.

Computers give visitors information about the museum and, in a fascinating but temporary exhibition likely to be moved to the Acropolis Study Centre at some stage, computers also give animated displays of construction techniques used in building the Parthenon.

On the corner of Irodotou and Vasilissis Sofias is the entrance to the new wing (added in 1992) of the Cycladic Museum, joined to the main building by a glass-covered walkway. This wing is as interesting for the building that houses it as for its contents. It was designed by and was the home of the German architect Ernst Ziller, the man also responsible for the Olympic Stadium, the Presidential Palace and Heinrich Schliemann's house on Panepistimiou. Some rooms of the museum display furniture and water-colours, giving an impression of the mansion's appearance when Ziller lived in it during the late 19th century. Other rooms contain an extension of the main Cycladic collection. There is a shop downstairs, and space upstairs for temporary exhibitions.

9
Pláka

It is hard to imagine anyone coming to Athens and not visiting the Pláka – always the hub of the city's eating and nightlife for locals and travellers alike.

It is hard to stroll the Pláka's streets without being reminded that you're a tourist, since they are lined with souvenir shops and every few doors you will find someone trying to entice you into their taverna. The Pláka is a tourist trap in many ways but, like Soho in London or the Left Bank in Paris, it is also where you'll find the locals eating and drinking. The area developed mainly in the 19th century on the north side of the Acropolis, when the population of Athens began to expand. As a result there are many fine buildings on view, and you can see inside some of these mansions. A few are still in their original state, such as the Centre for Hellenic Tradition (➤ 42); others have been modernised as museums, like the Kanellopoulos (➤ 53) or the Museum of Greek Musical Instruments (➤ 23).

Above all, the Pláka is a place for strolling and eating, day or night. There are countless restaurants here, some long-established and others more fly-by-night. Don't be tempted to eat in a particular place simply because someone is employed to stand outside and be affable. You may get a good meal, but the best places tend to exist because of their reputation among the Athenians themselves and therefore they don't need to tout for custom. All the places recommended under 'Where to Eat' (➤ 92–9) have been tried by the author, some of them many times over. Not one of them will overcharge or serve you second-rate 'tourist' fare.

🕂 57C2

🚇 Monastiráki

↔ Many Athens attractions are in and around the Pláka (➤ 56–7 Pláka map)

Old Pláka mansions have been adapted to the needs of modern visitors, as well as of local people

10
Stádio
(Olympic Stadium)

For sheer, simple grace, the beauty of this stone athletics stadium, within sight of the equally graceful Acropolis, is hard to beat.

The Stádio is the finishing point for the Athens marathon, run each October

➕ 29E1

✉ Leoforos Ardhittou

🕐 Daily sunrise–sunset

🍴 None

🚌 2, 4, 11, 12

♿ Few

✋ Free

↔ National Gardens (► 37), Presidential Palace (► 65), Temple of Olympian Zeus (► 55)

This stadium was built in 1896 when the Olympic Games were revived and fittingly held in their original home. Many Greeks were disappointed at not being awarded the 1996 Olympics, though they will be returning in 2004. The 1896 stadium is also named after the Panathenaic Stadium, where contests were held on this site from the 4th century BC onwards. The Olympic stadium follows the same plan as the ancient stadium, which was described by the geographer Pausanias in the 2nd century AD. Architect Ernst Ziller, responsible for many fine late 19th-century Athenian buildings, was commissioned to design the stadium in the spirit of its predecessor.

A visit to the stadium won't take long as there is little to see other than the structure as a whole, but you may find some Athenians jogging round the track, and visitors can wander around the centre and look at the statues marking starting and finishing points. Photographers will also be tempted by the sweeping curves and repetitive lines of the 47 rows of seats, which hold up to 60,000 spectators. The seating is on three sides only, leaving the fourth open with views across to one of the few wooded areas in central Athens, a corner of the National Gardens. The Stádio is not to be confused with the modern Olympic Stadium, which was built in 1982 in the northern suburbs.

What
to See

Above: icon from the
Byzantine Museum
Right: the National Guard
on duty at the Tomb of
the Unknown Soldier

27

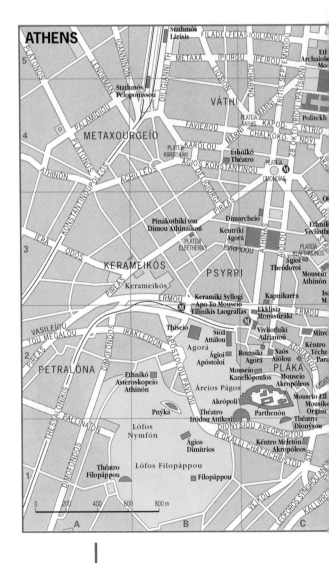

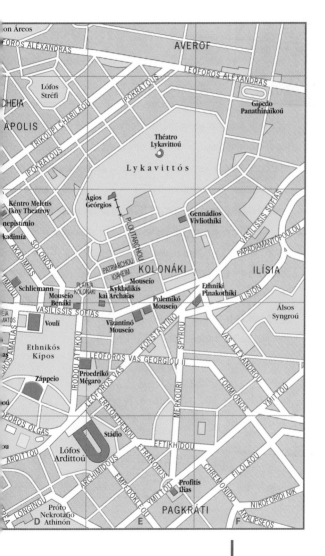

Athens

Although the area of Greater Athens covers 427sq km and, like any city today, it has its sprawling suburbs, most of the visitor attractions are in a small area within the city centre, mainly within easy walking distance of each other. Walking along some of the busy Athenian streets can be a noisy experience due to the heavy traffic, yet somehow this can help you appreciate what a remarkable city it is. Roads are diverted around little Byzantine churches, and the metro clanks past archaeological remains. Work had to be halted during construction of the new metro line when the engineers tried to tunnel beneath the Kerameikos Cemetery, only to find more remains far below those already uncovered. When you walk round Athens, you are just part of the latest layer of its long history.

'... Athens, diviner yet,
Gleamed with its crest of
columns, on the will
Of man, as on a mount of
diamond, set. '

PERCY BYSSHE SHELLEY
To Liberty (1819)

Athens

Many people choose cities for weekend breaks, and others will merely pass a day in Athens when on their way to the ever-popular Greek islands, but lucky are those who have several days in which to explore this multi-layered city. Athens is a Mediterranean city, a port, a city on the very edge of Europe, and a place with an extremely strong living culture, not merely a history. Enjoy it all.

The high notes of Athens are, of course its archaeological remains and the National Archaeological Museum (➤ 18–19), which displays the best finds from all over the Greek world. However, don't neglect the smaller museums, or the bustle of the real city on show in the flea markets and the Central Market (➤ 40). As in other Mediterranean countries, life here is lived on the streets, and the passing parade is as much a part of the appeal as the historical aspect. The Greeks invented drama, and still thrive on it. Athens may hit you – forcibly – as a very busy city indeed, and as in all capital cities people have less time for strangers than they do in the countryside. Don't be deceived, however. Athenians are natural talkers, hagglers and helpers. If you're lost, just ask – and then bear in mind that a Greek would rather give you the wrong answer than no answer at all! It's not that they don't like to admit their ignorance, more that they don't want to disappoint you by not being able to help.

Market stalls are a lively feature of this bustling city

What to See in Athens

57C1
Lysikratous
230
None

AGÍA AIKATERÍNI (CHURCH OF ST CATHERINE) ✪

Not far from the Monument of Lysikrates (➤ 48), in a small shady square fringed by small palm trees, stands the 11–12th-century church dedicated to St Catherine. It was given the name in 1769, when it was bought by the predominantly Greek Orthodox Monastery of St Catherine, in Egypt's Sinai desert. There are some later additions, obvious from the outside, and inside is a great deal of white marble, including a marble pulpit.

57C1
Kydathinaion
230
None

AGÍA SOTIRA (CHURCH OF ST SOTIRA) ✪

The main church of the Pláka district is opposite the entrance to the Museum of Greek Folk Art (➤ 22). Its full name is Sotira tou Kotaki and it was built in the late-11th and early-12th centuries, at the same time as the Church of St Catherine, a hundred metres away (see above). It has undergone many changes over the years, but in the grounds you can still see the fountain that was the only source of water in the Pláka until well after Greek Independence in the 19th century.

56B2
In the Agora site
Tue–Sun 8:30–2:45.
Closed public holidays
Theseion/Monastiráki
None
Expensive; free Sun

ÁGIOI APÓSTOLOI ✪✪
(CHURCH OF THE HOLY APOSTLES)

The site of one of the oldest churches in Athens is inside the Agora excavations and, though these are impressive enough, no visitor should miss looking inside this lovely church. It dates from AD 1000–25, but was much changed over the centuries. It was restored to its original form in

1954–6. The church was built above the ruins of a Roman nymphaeon (sanctuary of nymphs) from the 2nd century AD. The frescoes in the narthex (porch) are post-Byzantine and were moved here when the neighbouring church of Ágios Spyridon was demolished. The wall paintings in the church itself were found beneath the modern plaster.

ÁGIOS NIKODÍMOS (CHURCH OF ST NIKODIMOS) ✪

The original church on this site was built in AD 1031 and was a chapel for a Roman Catholic Monastery until 1701. It was pulled down in 1780 by the Turks and the bricks used for their Athenian defensive wall. In the 1850s the present church was built by the Russian Orthodox church, and it is still in use as Athens's main Russian Orthodox church. The imposing tower outside contains a bell that was donated by Tsar Alexander II, and which still makes a sound like thunder, as you will discover if you happen to pass by when it is rung. Inside the church, in addition to icons, there is some fine Russian embroidery.

ÁGIOS NIKÓLAOS RAGAVÁS (CHURCH OF ST NICHOLAS RAGAVAS) ✪

Right on the edge of the Anafiótika district (➤ 35) is the area's largest church, built in the 11th century. It was once part of the Palace of the prominent Rangavas family (which became Ragavas somewhere along the way), and indeed this whole area was once called Rangavas. If you look closely at the southeast side of the building you will see that it incorporates columns and other stonework from the Acropolis.

ÁGIOS PÁVLOS ✪ (CHURCH OF ST PAUL)

Not all the churches in Athens are Greek Orthodox; this handsome building, which has been recently restored, is the city's main Anglican church. When founded in 1838, it was in the middle of extensive gardens, but now it is surrounded by traffic at the busy junction of Filellinon and Amalias. Inside there are some lovely stained-glass windows showing St Paul, St Andrew and a story of the Life of David, among other biblical themes.

Opposite: the Church of St Catherine is dedicated to the saint who was tortured to death strapped to a wheel, hence 'Catherine Wheel'

✚ 57D2
✉ Filellinon
☎ 323-1090 (recorded message in Greek and Russian)
🚌 024, 230

✚ 57C1
✉ Prytaneiou/Epicharmou
☎ 322-8193
Ⓜ Monastiráki

The authoritative and pensive figure of a Greek priest in traditional garb

✚ 57D1
✉ Filellinon
🚌 024, 230
♿ None

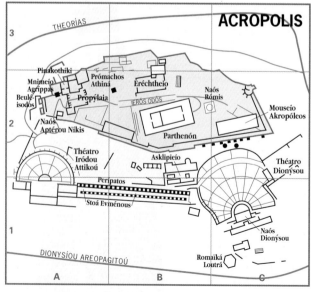

ACROPOLIS

THEORÍAS

Pinakothíki
Mnimeío Agríppas
Prómachos Athiná
Eréchtheio
Naós Rómis
Beulé-isodos
Propýlaia
IERÓS ODÓS
Mouseío Akropóleos
Naós Aptérou Níkis
Parthenón
Théatro Iródou Attikoú
Asklipieío
Théatro Dionýsou
Perípatos
Stoá Evménous
Naós Dionýsou
DIONYSÍOU AREOPAGITOÚ
Romaïká Loutrá

A   B   C

Did you know ?

Although millions of photographs are taken on the Acropolis every year, it was rather different in the summer of 1839. French-Canadian photographer Pierre Gustave Joly de Lotbinière needed horses to carry his photographic equipment up to the semi-derelict Acropolis. He exposed ten daguerreotypes, two of which were published in 1841 and survive as the very first photographs taken here.

AGORÁ (► 16, TOP TEN)

AKROPÓLI (► 17, TOP TEN)

ANAFIÓTIKA   ✪✪

Finding this lovely area of Athens is like stumbling unexpectedly upon a Greek island village. In fact, location apart, that is just what it is. When King Otto wanted a palace built for himself after assuming the Greek throne in 1832, he was told that the best builders in Greece came from the Cycladic island of Anafi, to the east of Thíra (Santorini). Once summoned, the builders knew they would be away for several years, and so they recreated their island home, complete with white cube houses and donkey-wide paths, at the foot of the Acropolis. By far the best way to approach the Acropolis is through Anafiótika, where charming home-made signs point the way and prevent you wandering into someone's garden by mistake.

ÁREIOS PÁGOS (AREOPAGOS)   ✪

Almost opposite the Acropolis entrance, some stone steps carved in the rock next to a plaque lead up to the Areopagos. This is where the supreme court of Athens once stood. The name means the Hill of Mars, and the legend is that here Mars (Ares to the Greeks), the God of War, was tried for murdering one of the sons of Poseidon. It is also where Orestes stood accused of murdering his mother, Clytemnaestra, in the Aeschylus play *Eumenides*. It was from the Areopagos that St Paul delivered his sermon to the Athenians in AD 54, and the text is inscribed on the plaque near the steps. The site has open access and is more noted for its views than for its few ancient remains.

Opposite: *sunlight paints the Acropolis gold, aided by minerals in the marble from which it was built*

🕂 57C1
🚌 230

Below: *some of the words from St Paul's sermon to the Athenians*

🕂 56B2
🕓 Open access
🚇 Monastiráki /Theseion
♿ None
🎟 Free

+ 57C2
✉ Nikis 39
☎ 322-5582
🕐 Mon–Fri 10–2:30, Sun
   10–2. Closed Sat, Greek
   and Jewish public
   holidays
🚇 Syntagma when opened
♿ Not known
✋ Free

EBRAÏKÓ MOUSEÍO TIS ELLÁTHOS ✪✪
(JEWISH MUSEUM OF GREECE)

This fascinating museum was closed at the time of writing, as it was being transferred to its new premises on the edge of the Pláka. Previously the contents were spread through several rooms, beginning with the ancient biblical origins of the arrival of Judaism in Greece in about the 2nd century BC. This is followed by a celebration of Jewish culture and its colourful costumes and ends with the dreadful years of the Holocaust, which completely wiped out many Greek Jewish communities, such as those in Kastoria, Crete and Drama. Only larger communities, such as those in Athens and Thessaloniki, survived, and even those only barely. The museum also contains a 1920s synagogue, moved here from Patra, reconstructed and rededicated. A small shop sells postcards and a good selection of books covering Jewish history in Greece.

+ 57C1
✉ Kydathinaion 14
☎ 331-2995
🕐 Mon–Wed 9:30–1:30,
   Fri 9:30–1:30, 5–8,
   Sat–Sun 10–1. Closed
   Tue, Thu, public
   holidays
🚇 Syntagma when opened
♿ None
✋ Free

ELLINIKO PAITHÍKO MOUSEÍO ✪✪
(HELLENIC CHILDREN'S MUSEUM)

This is an enjoyable new venture, although small and a little improvised as yet. Its maze of rooms includes work rooms, play rooms and displays on such subjects as the building of the new Athens metro lines. This allows children to don hard hats and wield shovels as they do their bit to speed up the metro's progress. Other fun activities include the ancient (dressing up in old clothes) to the modern (a computer). Contact the museum for current details. Although some of the staff speak English and other languages, and welcome all children, advance notice for visits by non-Greek-speaking children is advisable.

This little boy would soon be cheered by the delights of the children's museum (right)

ETHNIKÍ PINAKOTHÍKI (NATIONAL GALLERY) ✪

This is not well signposted, but is the ugly block of a building opposite the rather more attractive-looking Hilton Hotel. As a National Gallery it is disappointing compared to equivalent galleries in other European capitals. But it is worth visiting to see the work of Greek artists, including five paintings by perhaps the greatest of them all, El Greco. Some older Greek land- and seascapes are enjoyable for those who know the country, regardless of their artistic merit. Other European artists represented include Picasso, Brueghel, Rembrandt, Goya, Caravaggio and Van Dyck, but not even this small collection is permanently on display. The Gallery proper, only accessible through the front rooms where temporary exhibitions are held, closes while exhibitions are mounted or dismantled.

ETHNIKÓ ARCHAIOLOGIKO MOUSEÍO (NATIONAL ARCHEOLOGICAL MUSEUM) (➤ 18, TOP TEN)

ETHNIKÓS KÍPOS (NATIONAL GARDENS) ✪

Also known as the Royal Gardens, these were created in the 1840s under the direction of Queen Amalia, wife of Otto, the first King of Greece. They cover 16ha and offer a shady, peaceful retreat from the noisy city streets: ponds filled with fish and terrapins, tree-lined paths, fountains, cafés and children's play areas. Other attractions include a children's library and a small Botanical Museum. Less pleasing are stray cats and a sad attempt at a zoo. At the southern end stands the Zappeion, built in the late 19th century by two wealthy Greek-Romanians as an exhibition hall, and now used as a conference centre.

+ 29F3
✉ Vasileos Konstantinou 50
☎ 723-5937, 721-1010
🕐 Mon, Wed–Sat 9–3; Sun 10–2. Closed public holidays
🚌 234
♿ None
✋ Moderate

Queen Amalia ordered her Navy to bring seedlings from Italy for the National Gardens (below and inset)

+ 29D2
🕐 Daily sunrise–sunset
🍴 Cafés (£)
🚌 2, 4, 11, 12
✋ Free

29D4
Many (£–££)
Omonia

EXÁRCHEIA (EXARCHIA) ✪

This neighbourhood has long been the local hang-out for students, and came to the eyes of the world on 17 November 1973, when students occupied the Polytechnic in protest against more than six years of dictatorship by the Colonels. After several days the Colonels sent in the tanks, killing an unknown number of students and beginning the end of their own downfall. The Polytechnic building, at the junction of 28 Oktovriou and Stournari, still bears some of the scars. Walk up Stournari to the lively little Exarchia Square, filled with bars and cafés, for a feel of the area. At night the streets are livelier still, with more bars and *ouzeries* opening up and quickly filling – to remain full until the early hours.

28B1
Cafés (£)
230
None

FILOPÁPPOU (PHILOPAPPOU) ✪✪

In the Pnyka (➤ 63) and on top of the Hill of the Muses (147m) is the Monument of Philopappou. Banished to Athens by the Romans, Philopappou became the Roman Consul in Athens in AD 100. He was popular here because of his generosity and was allowed to build this grandiose tomb on one of the city's prime sites in AD 114–6.

The unusual towering form of the Monument of Philopappou

29E3
Soudias 61
721-0536
Mon–Tue, Fri 9–5,
Wed–Thu 9–8, Sat 9–2.
Closed public holidays,
August
3, 7, 8, 13
None
Free

GENNÁDIOS VIVLIOTHÍKI (AMERICAN SCHOOL OF ✪ CLASSICAL STUDIES)

This neo-classical building in Kolonáki houses an extensive library on Greek subjects, founded by John Gennadios and opened in 1926. It contains over 24,000 books, though its main interest to the visitor to Athens is likely to be the small collections of Byron (➤ 14) memorabilia and Edward Lear paintings. Byron's belongings are in a small case to the far left as you enter, and include his watch and some papers. Lear's work is on display on the walls, including the gallery accessed by stairs near the entrance.

HEPHAISTEION
(TEMPLE OF HEPHAISTOS)

✪✪✪

This fine temple dominates the western side of the Agora
(➤ 16). It is also known as the Thiseío (Theseion) – as is
the surrounding area of Athens – because some of its
friezes show Theseus, one of the mythical Kings of Athens
and son of Aegeus, after whom the Aegean Sea is named.
Hephaistos was god of fire and art as well as god of metal-
lurgy and, just as the potters' quarter was at nearby
Keramikos (➤ 45), so this was the blacksmiths' and metal-
workers' area. The temple was built in about 449–444 BC,
and the start of its construction launched the Golden Age
of Pericles (➤ 14). It is easily the best-preserved building
in the Agora, if not one of the best in all of Greece.

✚ 56A2
✉ In the Agora, Adrianou
   24
☎ 321-0185
🕐 Tue–Sun 8:30–2:45.
   Closed public holidays
🚇 Theseion/Monastiráki
♿ None
🍴 Expensive; free Sun

ISTORIKÓ MOUSEÍO
(NATIONAL HISTORICAL MUSEUM)

✪

This archive of historical documents and artefacts is
displayed in the former Greek Parliament building, built in
1858 and home to the Parliament until 1934. Indeed, one
of the chief attractions is the chance to see the grand
Debating Hall of the Old Parliament. The museum is likely
to be mainly of interest to historians, while admirers of
Lord Byron (➤ 14) will find a room containing some of his
belongings, such as his sword, desk, trunk, pistol and
helmet. The rooms tell the story of modern Greek history,
from about the 14th century until shortly after independence. There is a large collection of weaponry, and tributes
to the freedom fighters who helped Greece gain its
independence. As expected, it is very Greek centred, with
numerous paintings of Greek worthies. Unfortunately, only
summarised information is available in anything other than
Greek (English and French).

✚ 28C3
✉ Stadiou 13
☎ 323-7617
🕐 Tue–Sun 9–1:30. Closed
   public holidays
🚇 Plateía Syntagmatos
   when opened
♿ None
🍴 Moderate

Above: *the temple
dedicated to Hephaistos,
who made the armour
for Achilles*

39

28C3
Ermou/Kapnikareas
322-4462
Monastiráki
None

*Shops and stalls in and
around the Central
Market specialise in one
or two items, here nuts
and brandy*

KAPNIKARÉA

In 1834, when Ermou Street was built, there was talk of
destroying this delightful Byzantine church, which stands
right in the middle of the long, straight road opposite the
Parliament Building. Thankfully Ludwig of Bavaria, father of
Otto, the first King of the Greeks, intervened, and the
church was saved. The present building dates back to the
13th century, though there was a church here as long ago
as the 11th century. Since 1931 it has belonged to the
University of Athens, who helped to restore it. Inside, the
walls are lined with paintings, though they can be hard to
distinguish unless the day is very sunny.

28C3
Athinas/Evripidou
Mon–Sat early to late
Several nearby (£)
Omonia

KENTRIKÍ AGORÁ (CENTRAL MARKET)

To the south of Omonia, where Athinas meets Evripidou,
is the 19th-century metal structure that houses the city's
main meat and fish markets. This bustles with business six
days a week, and inside you will find every type of fish
from the Aegean and beyond, and every cut of meat
you're likely to find on a Greek plate. It is not a place for
vegetarians to linger. Instead, they may wish to explore
the streets which radiate from here, where other markets
and fascinating shops can be found, displaying fruit,
vegetables, flowers, nuts, spices, olives, cheese and much
more. On a sunny day, photographers can be seen taking
shot after shot of the rainbow-coloured displays. It is
definitely the place to visit to see Athenians bartering, and
to buy something tasty to take home. It is also the place to
go if you're planning a picnic for a day out.

Markets & Bazaars

Starting in Monastiráki Square, walk slightly downhill along the main road, Ermou.

On Sundays this is lined with junk stalls, and on weekdays furniture and other shops are open. To your left is the Monastiráki bazaar area (➤ 50), busy every day.

Go straight ahead through the traffic lights and on your right you reach the boundary fence for the Kerameikós Cemetery (➤ 45).

Food, drinks, fruit and bric-à-brac for sale outside Monastiráki metro station

To visit this continue walking – the entrance is on your right. On Sundays this area is packed with market stalls.

If not visiting the cemetery, turn right where the wall begins, along Melidoni.

On your right is a synagogue.

Turn left at the end, taking the second right – Psaromilingon. Cross the small square and continue along Korinis.

You are now heading for the old market area of Athens, down narrow streets where shops selling nuts, bread, spices and other goods are plentiful.

At the end of Korinis turn right (Sapfous), left (Menandrou) and finally right along Sofokleous.

Sofokleous is another street at the heart of the trading centre, with specialist shops and wholesalers bustling at peak times.

When you reach Athinas, turn right.

Cross the road to visit the old Central Market (➤ 40), noted for meat and fish but also selling many other Greek foodstuffs. Vegetarians may prefer not to venture too far inside the meat and fish sections.

Continue down Athinas and back to Monastiráki Square.

Distance
2.5km

Time
1 hour without stops, 2–3 hours with visits

Start/end point
Monastiráki Square
✠ 56B2
Ⓜ Monastiráki

Lunch
Sigalas (£)
✉ Plateía Monastiráki 2
☎ 321-3036

41

This loom is part of the weaving display in the Centre for Popular Arts and Traditions

KÉNTRO ELLINIKIS PARADOSIS (CENTRE FOR HELLENIC TRADITION)

Up some stairs in an arcade between Mitropoleos and Pandrossou is this excellent outlet for Greek artists and craftsmen working in traditional styles. Here you can find furniture, jewellery, ceramics, hand-painted signs, paintings, embroidery and all manner of ideas for good-quality souvenirs. On the second floor are temporary arts and crafts exhibitions, and another display area where more expensive antiques are for sale. On the first floor is also a very good café and restaurant.

KÉNTRO LAIKIS TÉCHNIS KAI PARADOSIS (CENTRE FOR POPULAR ARTS AND TRADITIONS)

The street on which this Pláka mansion stands is named after its former occupant, Angeliki Hatzimikali, who was born in 1895. She was an artist, writer, arts patron and lover of Greek folk art. Her home is as fascinating for itself as for the items on display from the collection of the Greek Folklore Society: silverwork, costumes, agricultural tools, paintings, pottery and textiles.

KÉNTRO MELETIS IKOY THEATROY (GREEK THEATRE MUSEUM)

In the basement rooms below the Greek Cultural Centre – call in to get a programme of current cultural events in the many state-owned museums and galleries – is this small, but fun, museum devoted to Greek theatre. Unless you are especially interested and can read the Greek captions, it will probably not detain you for long, but it has some enjoyable exhibits. The most interesting section is the row of re-created dressing rooms of prominent Greek actors, including the much-loved Melina Mercouri (► 14). Her gowns, some books, shoes, glasses, make-up box, letters from fans and much other memorabilia are effectively displayed. The museum also contains theatrical costumes, puppets, posters and miniature stage sets from important Greek productions.

**KÉNTRO MELETÓN AKROPÓLEOS
(ACROPOLIS STUDY CENTRE) (➤ 20, TOP TEN)**

KERAMIKÍ SYLLOGÍ APO TO MOUSEÍO ✪✪✪
**ELLINÍKIS LAOGRAFÍAS (CERAMIC COLLECTION
OF THE MUSEUM OF GREEK FOLK ART)**

The mosque in which this enjoyable collection is housed
was built in 1759 on the site of a fountain. Since the state
of Greece was founded it has been a barracks for the army
band, and then a hospital. It specialises in ceramics from
Greece and Cyprus from the first half of the 20th century.
The 794-piece collection is part of that of Professor
Vassilios Kyriazopoulos, who built it up over 50 years.

One fascinating aspect of the museum is that it tells the
stories, in Greek and English, of some of the potters
whose work is on display. Minas Avramides, for example,
was an uneducated stonemason before becoming a potter
in Thessaloniki, where his son still operates a workshop.
His drawings of men, gods and beasts are primitive, but
the finished plates have a colourful boldness. Avramides
also designed a Greek alphabet using animal motifs.
Nikolaos Yasiranis (1901–73) was from Rhodes, his father
having been a clay modeller in Asia Minor, from where
many of the craftsmen featured originated. The son's clay
models depicting characters from folk traditions are
delightful and amusing, showing a wicked eye for human
nature. In the gallery upstairs are small themed collections
from outside Greece, from Macedonia, Thessaly and from
the islands. The colourful decorated plates from Rhodes,
with their bold reds, blues and greens, are a typical
example. The white, bright interior of the mosque's dome
has been restored, but patches of the original, faded,
painted brickwork still show through.

*The Mosque of the Lower
Fountain*

➕ 56B2
✉ Tzami Tsistarakis,
Areos 1
☎ 324-2066
🕐 Wed–Mon 9–2:30.
Closed public holidays
🚇 Monastiráki
♿ None
▮ Moderate

Around the Acropolis

Distance
2km

Time
2–3 hours with stops

Start point
Monastiráki Square
🚇 56B2
🚊 Monastiráki

End point
Plateía Lysikrátous
🚇 57C1
🚌 230

Lunch/tea
Diogenes (££)
✉ Selley 3, Plateía
Lysikrátous
☎ 322-4845

Beginning in Monastiráki Square, walk up Areos towards the Acropolis.

On your left is the mosque housing the Ceramic Collection of the Museum of Greek Folk Art, which is well worth a visit (➤ 43). Just beyond are the remains of the Library of Hadrian.

At the end of Areos, turn left and then right, up Dioskoron. If in doubt at any time, walk up! At the end of Dioskoron, climb the steps which zigzag towards the Acropolis, sometimes so narrow that they seem to disappear.

On your right is the Agora (➤ 16). The temple you can see is the Theseion, which gives its name to the area around it. Further on is the Areopagos, and opposite on your left the entrance to the Acropolis (➤ 17).

If visiting the Acropolis, turn left as you leave it to walk down the steps up which the majority of tourists climb. At the bottom, as you turn left along Areopagitou, you will pass the lines of parked tourist buses.

On your left stands the Odeon of Herodes Atticus (➤ 55).

To visit this theatre take the path off to the left. Otherwise, continue along the road which then passes the entrance to the Theatre of Dionysos (➤ 68).

The original Library of Hadrian was much larger than the ruins suggest: 120m by 80m

Across the road on your right is the Acropolis Study Centre (➤ 20), still being developed and therefore looking like a building site.

If you wish to visit it, cross at the first traffic lights and the entrance is down Makriyanni. If not, turn left at the lights, along Vyronos (Byron Street) and up to the Plateía Lysikrátous for a restful break.

KERAMEIKÓS (KERAMIKOS CEMETERY) ✪✪

This principal cemetery of ancient Athens was in the Kerameikos, or potters' quarter of the city. Keramos was the patron saint of potters: hence, ceramics. The cemetery contains tombs and archaeological finds dating back to the 12th century BC, when it was first used for burial purposes. Many tombstones have been replaced as they were, lining the grand Street of the Tombs, which was reserved for the rich. One such, the Tomb of Dionysios of Kollytos, a wealthy Athenian treasurer, is marked by a fine statue of a powerful bull. Others range from the ostentatious to the simple but powerfully moving.

There is also abundant wildlife here, attracted by the stream that flows rather sluggishly through the grounds. Tiny terrapins can be seen in the grass, in the trees are chaffinches and black redstarts, while olive trees and other plants grow in profusion. It can be a peaceful haven from the traffic of the city, except on Sunday mornings when the noisy flea market takes place outside the walls.

The museum here is named after Gustav Oberlander, an industrialist who provided funds towards the excavation of the site in the 1930s. It contains good displays of the potter's art, as well as examples of *ostraka*, or voting tablets for Athenian elections, from which the term ostracism is derived. There are also some incredibly poignant gravestones, such as the one containing this message from a grieving father: 'This monument, Xenophantes, your father created for you on your death, Sophilos, for whom you, in parting, created sorrow'.

28B3
Ermou 148
346-3552
Tue–Sun 8:30–3. Closed public holidays
Theseion
None
Moderate

Most of the tombs in the Keramikos Cemetery date from about the 4th century BC

Designers both Greek and foreign congregate in Kolonáki, and window shopping is free

 29E2

234

Reservoir
If you walk directly towards Lykavittós from the northern corner of Kolonáki Square, you reach a small park named Dexameni. This means 'reservoir', for below your feet is the main water tank for supplying central Athens, on the site of a Roman reservoir.

KOLONÁKI ✪✪

The Kolonáki district is one of those areas of Athens which surprises many visitors. They expect the classical sites, the lively Pláka, the bustling bazaar areas, but somehow don't anticipate this chic and expensive part of the city, where designer clothes shops are frequented by wealthy widows, who walk their little dogs on the street for all the world as if they were in Paris. Here, too, are art galleries, stores selling the latest in mobile phones and other electronic goods, bars, *ouzeries*, pavement cafés and antiques shops whose prices will make you think it would be cheaper to buy a piece of the Parthenon.

The heart of the district is Plateía Kolonakíou, or Kolonáki Square. It may be expensive to sit outdoors here and have a coffee and a slice of gateau (if you have a sweet tooth then visiting the area's pastry shops is a must), but you will get value for money in watching the passers-by and the people sitting at neighbouring tables, reading newspapers or gossiping about the latest art trend or political scandal. If there were an export market in political scandals, Greece would certainly be a rich country!

The official name of the square is Plateía Filikís Eteriás, but no one calls it that. *Kolonáki* simply means a column, and if you look closely under the trees in the southwest corner of the square, you will see the small ancient column which gave its name first to the square and later to the whole district.

LYKAVITTÓS (LYKABETTOS HILL) (➤ 21, TOP TEN)

Around Kolonáki and Lykavittós

From Syntagma Square walk up Vasilissis Sofias, the main road to the left of the Parliament building. At the fifth junction on your left, on the corner with Koumbari, stands the Benaki Museum (▶ 51).

The museum houses the art collection of a wealthy Greek merchant, Antoine Benaki.

Turn left by the museum, up Koumbari to Kolonáki Square.

Kolonáki is one of the most fashionable districts of Athens, the kind of place where well-to-do Greek ladies walk their dogs. Kolonáki Square is surrounded by designer stores, cafés and smart gift shops.

Cross the square and leave it at the far right corner along the main road, Patriarchou Ioakim. Cross two junctions; at the third, at the first set of traffic lights, turn left up Plutarchou.

This steep street leads towards Lykabettos Hill (▶ 21), visible at the top.

At the end of Plutarchou you may appreciate taking the funicular to the top of Lykabettos Hill.

Enjoy the views over Athens: on a clear day you can see as far as the island of Aegina.

Take the zigzag path to the left, going down again through the lightly wooded slopes of the hill. If you ignore minor paths to left and right, you emerge on Aristippou, about 100m down from the funicular station. Head straight down Loukianou, another steep stepped Kolonáki Street, back down to Vasilissis Sofias, to emerge almost opposite the Byzantine Museum.

Turning left here would take you to the War Museum (▶ 64) and, near the Hilton Hotel, the National Gallery (▶ 37). If you have had enough walking for one day, turn right back down Vasilissis Sofias to Syntagma Square.

Distance
3km

Time
1½ hours without stops, 2–3 hours with stops

Start/end point
Plateía Syntagmatos

➕ 29D2

🚇 Syntagma, when opened

Lunch/tea
GB Corner (£££)

✉ Grande Bretagne Hotel, Syntagma Square

☎ 323-0251 ext 858

In summer the funicular takes people to the top of Lykavittós every ten minutes, but less frequently in winter

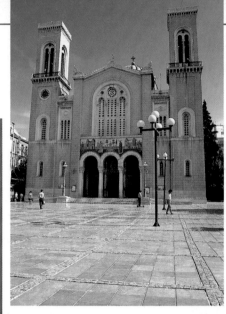

The first stone of the Cathedral of Athens was laid by King Otto and Queen Amalia on Christmas Day 1842

 57C2
☒ Plateía Mitropoleos
☺ Monastiráki
& None
⚕ Free

MITRÓPOLIS ✪✪

Two very contrasting churches stand side by side in Mitrópolis Square. The smaller is the Mikrí Mitrópoli (Little Mitrópoli), a 12th-century church dedicated to Ágios Eleftherios. It has a haunting cave-like atmosphere: do go in if you find it open. It is dwarfed by its huge neighbour, the Megáli Mitrópoli (Great Mitrópolis), the Cathedral of Athens, a modern building on the site of a monastery that stood in the square until 1827. The cathedral's main exterior feature is its fine entrance. Above this is a mosaic of the Annunciation (*Evangelismos*), which gives the church its official name.

✚ 57C1
☒ Plateía Lysikrátous
🚌 1, 5, 9, 18

MNIMEÍO LYSIKRÁTOUS ✪
(MONUMENT OF LYSIKRATES)

This unassuming marble monument, in a small square off the main Pláka streets, has a fascinating history. It was built in 334 BC and is the city's only complete surviving choregeic monument. These were built as tributes to the winners in an annual music and drama festival at the nearby Theatre of Dionysos (➤ 68). Lysikrates was the sponsor (*choregoi*) behind the winning team, as an inscription around the monument explains. The team was the chorus in a drama competition the previous year, and the monument originally included the tripod, which victors were traditionally awarded. There were once many such monuments around here, hence the name of the street, Tripodou. In more recent times, the six-columned building was converted by monks into a library, and it was while in the library in 1810 that Lord Byron (➤ 14) wrote some of his epic poem, *Childe Harold's Pilgrimage*.

Byzantine Churches of Athens

Starting in Mitrópolis Square, walk up the street left of the main cathedral.

On your right is the 16th-century chapel of Ágia Dynamis.

Go up to Syntagma Square and turn right along Filellinon. The tower of the Church of St Nikodimos (➤ 33) is visible.

To visit this Byzantine church, cross over the busy road. Further along is the Church of St Paul (➤ 33).

Cross back over Filellinon and look for the Museum of Greek Folk Art sign. Follow this down Kydathinaíon.

On your right is the 12th-century Byzantine church dedicated to the Transfiguration of Jesus Christ.

Further down Kydathinaíon is a small square surrounded by cafés. Cross this diagonally to the far right corner and walk down the short street.

Reach the 11th-century Church of St Catherine (➤ 32).

Past the church, turn right up Adrianou, then first left, climbing to the T-junction. Turn right.

This is Anafiótika (➤ 35), the area below the Acropolis.

Follow the narrow street and the signs for the Acropolis, past the church of St George on the Rocks and the 1774 church of Ágios Simeon.

This brings you to the site of the first university of the independent Greek state. It is now a small museum.

Turn right after the university down Klepsithras to the Roman Agora. Skirt right then left around the Agora, right down Eolou and right again up the pedestrianised Ermou.

Ahead is the Kapnikaréa (➤ 40), yet another of the many ancient churches that survive in the centre of Athens.

Pass Kapnikaréa and take the first right to return to Mitrópolis.

Distance
2.5km

Time
1 hour without stops, 2–3 hours with stops

Start/end point
Mitrópolis
✚ 28C2
Ⓜ Monastiráki

Tea
Kapnikarea Café (£)
✉ Christofolou 2
☎ 322-7394

The 'Little Mitrópolis' is officially known as the Church of the Panaghía Gorgoepiíkoös: the Madonna Who Swiftly Hears

Top: *colourful rugs in the Monastiráki areas*
Above: *the metro only has one north–south line, from Kifissia to Piraeus, but another is under construction*

MONASTIRÁKI ●●●

This small and ever-bustling square gets its name because a monastery once stood here. Anything less monastic today would be hard to imagine. As well as the busy metro station, where commuters with their briefcases rub shoulders with housewives visiting the markets and backpackers heading for the port of Piraeus, there are cafés and market stalls, and it's the hub of several areas.

To the west is the Monastiráki area itself, where the Pláka souvenir shops give way to the flea market. This is busy every day, but packed on Sunday mornings when it stretches along Ermou past the Keramikos Cemetery, making enough noise to wake its inhabitants. Stalls sell a bewildering variety of items, from cheap clothes and shoes to expensive cameras, from stuffed storks to *souvlaki* and from religious icons to pornographic videos. Visitors are advised to watch out for pickpockets, and to allow plenty of time for a visit as the street becomes so packed it is often almost impossible to move.

To the southeast of the square is the Pláka district, and to the northwest the newly fashionable neighbourhood of Psirri, where smart bars and restaurants are appearing among its old workshops.

MOUSEÍO ATHINÓN ●
(MUSEUM OF THE CITY OF ATHENS)

Despite being the original Royal Palace, home of King Otto between 1836 and 1842, this is an easily missed small white building on the south side of Plateía Klafthmonos. The refurbished royal apartments are surprisingly modest, and the walls display many prints and paintings of Athens over the years, including work by the British artists Edward Lear and J M W Turner. Also on display is King Otto's copy of the 1843 Greek Constitution, and there are changing exhibitions in the ground floor galleries.

MOUSEÍO BENÁKI (BENAKI MUSEUM) ✪✪✪

Quite when the improvements to the Benaki Museum will be finished is, as with most work in Greece, impossible to predict. The museum was closed in 1994. A planned reopening in 1996 became early 1998, and then early 1999, with the building still being worked on at the time of writing. The only part currently open is the museum shop, which looks smart and modern, which is a good omen for the rest of the work.

The collection of Greek and Egyptian items, as well as the the house in which they are displayed, belonged to an Alexandrian Greek cotton trader, Antoine Emmanuel Benaki (1873–1954). Over a period of 35 years he amassed a splendid selection of artefacts, which he eventually gave to the Greek state for display in a museum. The collection incorporates paintings (including an El Greco), jewellery from Mycenae, ceramics, icons, clothing and Greek folk art, such as bridal cushions, traditional clothing and decorative items. Lord Byron's writing desk is one of the many items from the War of Independence, along with other historical objects. A major attraction is a highly unusual piece: a complete Egyptian reception room from a palace of the 17th century. Another showcase item from Egypt, where Benaki made his great fortune, is a wonderfully sensitive portrait of a man, painted on linen in the 3rd century AD. The rooftop café is also well worth a visit.

✚ 29D2
✉ Vasilissis Sofias/Koumbari 1
☎ 361-1617
⊙ Reopens early 1999, details not yet confirmed
🍴 Café ££
🚌 023, 234

In addition to the items on display, the Benaki Museum also has a library of some 80,000 books available to scholars

MOUSEÍO ELLINIKÍS LAOGRAFIAS
(MUSEUM OF GREEK FOLK ART) (➤ 22, TOP TEN)

MOUSEÍO ELLINIKÍS PAITHIKIS TÉCHNIS ✪✪
(MUSEUM OF GREEK CHILDREN'S ART)

🕂 57D1
✉ Kodrou 9
☎ 331-2621
🕐 Tue–Sat 10–2, Sun
11–2. Closed public
holidays
🚇 Syntagma when opened
🚌 024, 230
♿ None
💰 Cheap; children and
students free

This smart new museum is a delightful idea, being
devoted to displaying and encouraging the artistic work of
Greek children, though overseas visitors with children will
be equally welcomed. The museum began as a private
collection of Greek children's art, which was originally on
display in the Milies Museum on the Pilion peninsula, but
has recently been brought to Athens and expanded. There
are some enchanting displays of paintings, small sculptures and puppets, all showing the original and vivid
imagination which can only come from a child. The main
paintings are inspired by annual competitions on themes
such as Greece and the Sea, Mother and Child, designing
a Greek stamp or telling a Greek folk tale, with the winning
paintings all being for sale. If you cannot afford an original,
many of them have been turned into notes
and postcards for sale in the small shop.

The gallery is upstairs, while downstairs
are bright and lively rooms, with painting
and drawing equipment and puzzles,
where regular activity sessions are held. If
you don't speak Greek but would like to
visit or would like your child to join in, then
a phone call in advance will ensure that an
English-speaking helper is on hand. Other
languages are not yet available, but ring to
check as the museum is slowly expanding
its activities – and quite rightly too.

MOUSEÍO ELLINIKÓN MOUSIKON
ORGÁNON (MUSEUM OF GREEK
MUSICAL INSTRUMENTS) (➤ 23,
TOP TEN)

*Look for this sign for the Museum of Greek
Children's Art, and uncover an El Greco of
the future?*

MOUSEÍO KANELLÓPOULOS (KANELLOPOULOS MUSEUM) ✪✪

This neo-classical mansion in the Pláka is easily visited while walking up to the Acropolis, and well merits a lengthy look. The house itself was built in 1884 and has been renovated to show off the private collection, put together over the years by Paul and Alexandra Kanellopoulos and now owned by the Greek government. The collection is very well displayed on several floors, with information available in Greek and English, although more details about specific objects rather than general descriptions of the contents of each case would be welcome.

As with any private collection it is eclectic, and this one ranges from the sacred to the profane. The latter is represented by erotic carvings of satyrs chasing, and sometimes catching, nymphs around the typical Greek red-on-black vases, which were being made in Athens in the 7th century BC. The sacred is represented by an extensive collection of icons on the ground floor. There is also some Mycenean gold and examples of arts and crafts by the Minoans, the Phoenicians and from Egypt, Italy and elsewhere. The collection covers the 3rd century BC to the 19th century. Note the huge block of stone on the ground floor, which fell from the Acropolis. There is some intricate Persian jewellery, and bead and glass work. Statues are also a feature, as is a fine bust of Alexander the Great.

🚼 56B1
✉ Panos/Theorias
☎ 321-2313
🕐 Tue–Sun, 8:30–3.
  Closed public holidays
🚇 Monastiráki
♿ None
✋ Moderate

The Neo-Classical Pláka mansion housing the Kanellopoulos Museum (below), and some of its exquisitely – and sometimes erotically – painted vases (inset)

56B1
Kallisperi 12
922-1044
Mon, Thu–Sat 9–4, Wed 9–9, Sun 10–4. Closed public holidays
Café/restaurant (££)
230
Excellent
Expensive

MOUSEÍO KOSMÍMATOS ILÍA LALAOÚNIS (ILIAS LALAOUNIS JEWELLERY MUSEUM) ○○

Ilias Lalaounis is one of the most famous of modern Athenian jewellers and goldsmiths, and a look around this museum, purpose-built in his old workshop, will explain why. This versatile artist and craftsman takes inspiration from many sources: Mycenean, Minoan, Byzantine, Viking, Persian and Celtic art, science and more. There are over 3,000 pieces on permanent display, beautifully lit and well captioned in Greek, English and French. A small theatre shows a choice of six short films on his techniques and particular collections, again in all three languages. There are also some delightful works based on designs submitted by children: giant bees and spiders, huge ants and locusts, spaceships, comets colliding, serpents and signs of the zodiac. The museum has a roof garden with views of the Acropolis, a café/restaurant and a well-stocked shop.

MOUSEÍO KYKLADIKIS KAI ARCHAÍS ELLENIKIS TÉCHNIS (GOULANDRIS MUSEUM OF CYCLADIC ART) (► 24, TOP TEN)

56B2
Pelopidha/Eolou
324-5220
Tue–Sun 8:30–2.45. Closed public holidays
Monastiráki

NAÓS AIÓLOU (TOWER OF THE WINDS) ○○

This, the best feature in the Roman Agora site (► 67), can be seen easily from outside the fencing, but you should take a closer look. The curious octagonal building dates from about 40 BC. One of its many features was a water clock, driven by a stream from the Acropolis; it still has its weather vane, compass and sundials, and a frieze depicting the eight wind gods. One of these, Ailos, gives his name to Eolou Street, on which the tower stands.

The unusual octagonal Tower of the Winds

ODION (THÉATRO) IRÓDOU ATTIKOU (ODEON OF HERODES ATTICUS) ⭐⭐

This splendid theatre on the southern slopes of the Acropolis was built in AD 161–174 by Tiberius Claudius Atticus Herodes, a wealthy businessman from Marathon, in memory of his wife Rigilla. As well as being the Roman Consul here, Atticus Herodes was a great patron of the arts, who erected many public buildings in Athens. A good view of the theatre, which seats 5,000, can be had from within the Acropolis itself, though the Odeon is only normally open during the Athens Festival, when it makes a dramatic setting for the drama and music on stage. When first built the theatre had a wooden roof, white marble seating and a mosaic floor. It was restored after World War II, and has been used by the Athens Festival since 1955. It is known locally as the Herodeion.

✚ 56B1
✉ Dionysiou Areopagitou
🕐 Open for Athens Festival and other occasional performances
🚌 230
♿ None

OLYMPÍEION (TEMPLE OF OLYMPIAN ZEUS) ⭐⭐

Known locally as Stíles Olympíou Díos, in its day this was the largest temple in Greece, its day being from about AD 130 onwards, when Emperor Hadrian completed work on it. He dedicated it to Olympian Zeus during the Panhellenic festival in AD 132. It was actually begun in the 6th century BC, with several unsuccessful attempts made to complete the massive project – the temple dwarfed the Parthenon and the Temple of Apollo at Delphi. The 15 columns that remain give a sense of the scale: there were originally 104 of them, each 17m high. One crashed spectacularly in 1852 and has been left where it fell. The columns look very impressive at sunrise, and when floodlit.

✚ 57D1
✉ Leoforos Olgas 1
☎ 922-6330
🕐 Tue–Sun 8:30–3. Closed public holidays
🚌 024, 230
♿ None
💶 Moderate

The Temple of Olympian Zeus has inspired painters such as Turner and writers such as Chateaubriand

PLÁKA

[map of Pláka district]

Hadrian's Arch, a former
gateway to ancient
Athens, stands 18m high

57C1
Leoforos Amalias
024, 230

PÍLI (PÝLI) ADRIANOÚ (HADRIAN'S ARCH) ✪✪

Along with the Acropolis and the adjacent Temple of
Olympian Zeus, Hadrian's Arch is one of the first ancient
sights visitors see when
reaching the city centre from
the airport. It tells you that
you are in a very old city –
literally so, as the inscription
on one side reads 'This is
Athens, the ancient city of
Theseus', and on the other,
'This is the city of Hadrian
and not of Theseus'. On the
Acropolis side of the Arch
you were in the ancient city,
and on the other side you
were in the modern Roman
version. Hadrian's marble
arch was built in the 2nd
century AD, roughly contemporaneous with the Temple
of Olympian Zeus.

PINAKOTHÍKI TOU DÍMOU ATHINAÏKOÚ (MUNICIPAL ART GALLERY) ⊘

Walk down the busy main street of Piraeus from Omonia Square and on your left you reach this under-rated modern Greek art collection, well worth knowing about if the National Gallery is closed. The gallery's building dates from 1872, when it was the Foundling Hospital, and the collection itself has been acquired since 1923. It covers a wide range of 19th- and 20th-century subjects, including evocative old street scenes and archetypal Greek landscapes, showing how the face of Greece has changed over the years. There are portraits of proud peasants, and examples of Greece's tradition of primitive artists. At the time of writing, the gallery was closed for alterations, so check before visiting this slightly out-of-the-centre location.

🞢 28B3
✉ Piraeus 51
🕐 Mon–Fri 9–1, 5–9, Sun 9–1. Closed public holidays
🚇 Omonia
💶 Free

Did you know ?

The origin of the Pláka district's name isn't known for sure. Pláka is the Greek word for a slab or a slate, and one theory is that it was named after a large stone slab found near the church of Ágios Yiorgios, near the Theatre of Dionysos.

PLÁKA (► 25, TOP TEN)

Through the Pláka

Distance
1.5km

Time
30 mins without stops, 2–3 hours with stops and shopping

Start point
Plateia Syntagmatos
✠ 57D2
Ⓜ Syntagma when opened

End point
Monastiráki Square
✠ 56B2
Ⓜ Monastiráki

Lunch
Five Brothers (£)
✉ Eolou 3
☎ 325-0088

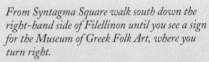

From Syntagma Square walk south down the right-hand side of Filellinon until you see a sign for the Museum of Greek Folk Art, where you turn right.

Kydathinaíon is one of the main Pláka streets, along with Adrianou and Pandrossou. On your left is the Museum of Greek Folk Art (▶ 22), and further along on your right the Hellenic Children's Museum (▶ 36).

Continue on down Kydathinaíon a short way and look on your right for Geronta.

At the far end of Geronta is the Centre for Popular Arts and Traditions (▶ 42), if you wish to make a detour.

Further down Kydathinaíon is the junction with Adrianou, but cross over and walk up Thespidou.

On the right you will find the studio of George Savakis, a Pláka artist who has painted many murals in the local tavernas as well as scenes of Pláka life.

Return to Adrianou and turn left to walk down into the shopping heart of the Pláka. After about 300m and beyond a small crossroads, look on the left for the small stepped street called Mnissikleous. Walk up here and take the first right, Diogenes.

Along Diogenes you will pass the well-known Platanos Taverna on the left, then the Museum of Greek Musical Instruments (▶ 23) on the right.

Diogenes brings you out at the Roman Agora (▶ 67). Turn right and walk round here, taking a right turn down Eolou. Pass Adrianou on your right and then take the next left, Pandrossou.

Yet another Greek snack is the doughnut: no one will starve while walking the streets of Athens

Pandrossou is another of the Pláka's shopping streets. If you turn right here you can walk up to Mitropóleos, but left takes you to the end of the walk in Monastiráki Square.

PLATEÍA KLAFTHMONOS (KLAFTHMONOS SQUARE) ⭐

This square off Stadiou literally means the Square of Wailing. Traditionally, civil servants from the many surrounding ministries come here to complain after being dismissed. At the bottom end stands the Byzantine Church of Ágioi Theodoroi (St Theodore), which was built in the 11th century and is one of the contenders for the oldest church in Athens. This is also the square where you will find the National Historical Museum (➤ 39).

🏛 28C3
✉ off Stadiou
🚇 Omonia

PLATEÍA OMONOÍAS (OMONIA SQUARE) ⭐

On some news-stands, among the picture postcards of Athens you occasionally find one of a picturesque Omonia Square, with a fountain and greenery in the centre and a few cars driving by. This is a very old postcard. For many years now the square has had numerous hoardings around it, behind which a great deal of building work has been going on. You will never find just a few cars driving by during daylight hours, at any time of the year, as this is one of the central traffic hubs. For most visitors Omonia will be a fume-filled noisy nightmare (ironically, its name means Harmony Square). It is a raucous reminder of the modern Athens that exists behind the picture postcards, with its metro station, fast-food joints, dubious hotels and even more dubious characters, including a recent influx of refugees from Albania and Eastern Europe, begging or selling cheap imported cigarettes and other goods. It may not be the prettiest aspect of Athens, but it remains a prominent and unavoidable face of this Balkan city.

🏛 28C4
🚇 Omonia

Lottery vendors, like this one on Omonia Square, are ex-soldiers supplementing their income

Food & Drink

It's easy to eat a poor meal in Athens – certain places in the Pláka spring to mind – but it is just as easy to make every meal a memorable one. Some places are low on sophistication, but great on atmosphere, price and hearty traditional food. There are hundreds of reliable medium-priced places too, and an ever-increasing number of new restaurants with chefs attempting to blend traditional Greek cooking with the latest world trends.

When to Eat

Greeks tend to eat late, and they seldom eat light. Restaurants are usually open from about noon onwards for lunch, and from seven o'clock for supper, but that is usually to catch the tourist trade – owners know the Athenians will not be out in force for some time. Many of the day's specials are prepared in the morning or at lunchtime, and a dish such as *moussaka* may be served lukewarm rather than piping hot – but that is the Greek way. If you like hot food, eat early or order something that you know has to be freshly prepared.

For Starters

Everyone knows about *taramasalata* and *tzatziki*, but there are many other enticing starters. A dip made from aubergines, *melitzanasalata*, is delicious, while a plate of feta cheese is another Greek favourite. Deep-fried, when it is called *saganaki*, it is excellent. Florina peppers are sweet red peppers, marinated, baked and served cold: and they look as good as they taste!

Above: little kebabs are popular snacks on the streets of Athens
Inset: try sampling a few different brands in one of the city's ouzeries

What to Drink

The Greek aperitif is ouzo, an aniseed-flavoured clear spirit that turns milky with water. Ouzo is always served with a glass of water, and sometimes with a small plate of

nibbles too. Greeks tend to drink ouzo neat, with a sip of water afterwards, rather than mix the two.

The Greeks don't drink a lot of wine, even though the country is renowned for its unique resinated white wine, retsina. Athenians out for a meal may well have beer and soft drinks, which is one reason for Greek wines' lack of renown. More recently, however, encouraged by the demands of visitors and the increasing sophistication of Athenian palates, Greek wine-makers have responded with an improvement in quality and some award-winning products. Look for labels with names such as Boutari, Tsantalis, Kourtakis and Domaine Carras, the country's leading producers.

After a meal it is common to drink a Greek brandy, although this is often done in a bar or at a pastry shop rather than in the restaurant. The brand name Metaxa is so dominant that it has become synonymous with the word 'brandy'. If you like your brandy smooth it is wise to choose the most expensive type, the 7-star Metaxa. Fewer stars generally mean a rougher drink.

Nuts and olives like this are very tempting to Athenians, who love to nibble

The ubiquitous and healthy Greek salad is more commonly known to the Greeks themselves as a peasant's salad or country salad

✚ 29D2
🚇 Metro station under construction

Above: *Syntagma Square is at last returning to its former pleasant looks*
Below: *the renovated beux-arts Grande Bretagne Hotel*

PLATEÍA SYNTAGMATOS (SYNTAGMA SQUARE) ✪✪✪

The main square of Athens, Constitution Square, is one that every visitor should see – and at some point probably will. The airport bus brings you here and picks you up again; there is a tourist information kiosk, a main post office, newspaper kiosks selling foreign papers, banks and currency exchanges. On one side is the distinguished Grande Bretagne Hotel, almost a tourist attraction in its own right. Richard Athauss, Elizabeth Taylor and Sir Winston Churchill have been among the guests. Churchill would have remembered the experience as it was during

World War II and an attempt was made on his life there! The hotel was built in 1862 as an annex to what was then the royal family's summer palace and is now the Greek Parliament Building, or Vouli, at the top of the square. In front of this is the Tomb of the Unknown Soldier, guarded by the Greek soldiers known as Evzones, whose Changing of the Guard ritual is one of the most popular tourist attractions. It is an impressive, precise and dramatic routine, with the guards dressed in their colourful traditional costumes. For the last few years the square has been almost sealed off and blighted by builders' hoardings while the new metro station has been under construction, but at the time of writing some of the hoardings have started to clear and the centre of Syntagma is turning back into the pleasant open space it once was – though the metro still has no firm completion date.

PNÝKA (PNYX)

⚫⚫

This green and hilly retreat is across the road from the Acropolis, yet few tourists take in this fascinating part of the city. Most visitors are ferried to the Acropolis in coaches and do not have the time, or inclination, to head in the opposite direction. The Pnyx itself is where, in the golden days of Periclean Athens, the Assembly would meet in the 18,000-seat amphitheatre (now filled with seating for *son et lumière*), and crowds would gather to hear the great orators of the day.

To the left of the main path, as you walk up beyond the entrance signs, a side path leads to the so-called 'Prison of Socrates'. Visitors should not get too excited, as these two holes in the wall look more like the entrances to a modern public lavatory and there is no historical evidence whatsoever to suggest that this was the prison where the philosopher Socrates was kept after being arrested for allegedly corrupting Athenian youth with his teachings. He was sentenced to death by drinking hemlock and actually died in the state prison in the Agora.

To the right of the main entrance path to the Pnyx, almost opposite the Prison of Socrates, is a Tourist Pavilion set in the trees. In front of the pavilion is a delightful, small church, Ágios Demetrius Loumbardiaris. This was originally built in 1460 and sympathetically rebuilt in 1955. Behind the church and Tourist Pavilion is the Pnyx itself, though access is limited because of its use for the *son et lumière* shows. Further on is the Hill of the Nymphs, also fenced off at the top because it houses an observatory.

☩ 28B2
🍴 Cafés (££)
🚌 230
♿ None

Did you know ?

On 26 October 1656, the feast of Saint Demetrius, the commander of the Turkish garrison on the Acropolis planned to fire his cannons on the congregation in the church on the Pnyx. At the crucial moment the Acropolis was struck by lightning, blowing up the explosives – and the commander. The church was named after the Turks' largest cannon, the Bombardier (or Loumbardiaris *in Greek).*

The Pnyx set for the dramatic sound and light show that tells the history of Greece and of the Acropolis

✚ 29E2

✉ Leoforos Vasilissis
Sofias 22/Rizari 2

☎ 729-0543

🕐 Tue–Fri 9–2, Sat–Sun
9:30–2. Closed public
holidays

🍴 Café (£)

🚌 234

♿ None

👆 Free

*The War Museum was
opened in 1975 shortly
after the last battles in
Greece, fought against
the military dictatorship
of the Colonels*

POLEMIKÓ MOUSEÍO   ✪✪
(WAR MUSEUM OF GREECE)

Don't be put off by the name or by the military hardware
outside this museum, for inside is a fascinating collection
covering many aspects of Greek history. As just one
example of its all-encompassing brief, it includes copies of
some dramatic friezes from the remote Temple of Vassai
on the Peloponnese, regarded as one of the most
outstanding Greek temples outside Athens. The friezes
show military conflict, and art lovers will appreciate
stumbling across such skilful replicas of otherwise
relatively inaccessible pieces.

The museum covers conflicts dating back to the Greek
myths, the Trojan Wars and the tales of Homer. There are
first-class models of many of the fortified towns in Greece,
such as Náfplio (► 84) and Mystras, and others showing
great battle scenes from Greek history. World War II is
covered in some depth, including the Battle of Crete and
the sufferings of the Athenian population. There is also an
extensive collection of weaponry and uniforms. Outside
the museum is a display of military vehicles. Children will
enjoy climbing up to peer inside the cockpits of the
Spitfires and Tiger Moths, and getting a close look at the
anti-aircraft guns and some fairly primitive World War I
hardware. Having examined the outside displays, go inside
and take the stairs or lift to the top floor, working your way
down, though the layout on the several floors is not strictly
chronological. This makes more sense of a visit, though,
and you may wish to take a break in the café in the
basement afterwards.

PROEDRIKÓ MÉGARO (PRESIDENTIAL PALACE) ✪

The present-day home of the Greek President was once the Royal Palace, until the Greek monarchy was officially abolished after a Referendum in 1974, following the overthrow of the Greek Colonels' military regime. The palace was constructed in 1878, yet another example of the many fine Athenian buildings designed by architect Ernst Ziller. It was restored in 1935, when it also became home to the Greek Parliament. Although it is closed to the public, it is worth strolling by to see the frontage, the guards on duty outside and, over the wall, a glimpse into the extensive gardens.

🔴 29D2
✉ Irodou Attikou
🕐 Closed to the public
🚇 Syntagma when opened
🚌 3, 7, 8, 13

One of the evocative statues to be found in the First Cemetery

PRÓTOÍ NEKROTAFÍO ATHINÓN (FIRST CEMETERY OF ATHENS) ✪✪

The First Cemetery is not called that because it is the oldest, but because it is the most important cemetery. Here distinguished citizens have a right to be buried, but there is room for more ordinary monuments too. Look for a moving carving of an old man and his wife, her arm resting gently on his – an affectionate portrait of a long-married couple. One of the graves most interesting to visitors is that of the archaeologist Heinrich Schliemann. It can be found on a small mound beyond the chapel, which is to the left as you enter. Schliemann's tomb was designed by his architect friend Ernst Ziller, who also designed the Presidential Palace, Olympic Stadium, Schliemann's House and other distinguished buildings in Athens. Also in the First Cemetery is the tomb of Theodoros Kolokotronis, the guerrilla leader hero of the Greek War of Independence, and prominent modern citizens, such as the actress/politician Melina Mercouri (➤ 14).

🔴 29D1
✉ Anapafsios
🕐 Daily 7–7
🚌 4
♿ Few
💲 Free

Modern Athens

Distance
5km

Time
1 hour without stops, 2–3 hours with stops

Start/end point
Plateía Syntagmatos

 29D2

Syntagma when opened

Lunch
Palia Athina (£)

Nikis 46

324-5777

Syntagma Square is the focal point of Athenian life, for celebrations, commemorations, public holidays and parades

At the top of Syntagma Square is the Greek Parliament Building. Walk to the left of this up Vasilissis Sofias.

On your left is the Benaki Museum (➤ 51) and the sign for the Goulandris Museum of Cycladic Art. On the right are the Byzantine (➤ 69) and War Museums (➤ 64).

Opposite the entrance to the Hilton Hotel, turn left up Gennadiou to the Gennadios Library (➤ 38).

The Library is mainly of interest to bibliophiles and admirers of Lord Byron (➤ 14).

From the bottom of Gennadiou, walk back towards Syntagma slightly to cross the junction. Walk diagonally down Vasilissis Konstantinou.

On the far side of the road is the National Gallery (➤ 37), whose collection includes modern Greek art.

Continuing down Vasilissis Konstantinou look for the right-hand turning down Vasilissis Giorgiou, which brings you out on Attikou with the Presidential Palace on your left.

Turn left round the front of the Palace to see the royal Guards in their traditional uniforms.

Continue down this street and the splendid Olympic Stadium (➤ 26) appears on your left.

Walk around the stadium – or even jog as Athenians do.

Cross the road opposite the entrance and veer to the left through the edge of the National Gardens.

On your right is the Zappeion, used for conferences.

Walk to the left of the Zappeion, turn left and then right, through a small gate to explore more of the National Gardens (➤ 37). The main road on your far left is Amalias. Return to this when ready and turn right to Syntagma.

ROMAÏKI AGORÁ (ROMAN AGORA) ✪

This is one of the few archaeological sites in Athens that is scarcely worth the price of admission. Its chief feature is the Tower of the Winds (➤ 54), which can, in any case, easily be seen from outside the walls. Apart from this, the mainly ground-level ruins are somewhat diminished by weeds and the packs of cats and dogs which have taken up residence. The small, attractive Fethiye Mosque, built in 1458 and dedicated by Sultan Mehmet II, is nowadays surrounded by lovely orange trees, but only used as a storeroom. Opposite the site entrance are the remains of a Medresse, an Islamic seminary which was destroyed by Greeks rebelling against the Turks during the War of Independence. It had been a prison and the tree in the courtyard was used for hangings.

➕ 56B2
✉ Pelopidha/Eolou
☎ 324-5220
🕐 Tue–Sun 8:30–2:45.
Closed public holidays
Ⓜ Monastiráki
♿ None
 Moderate

Fine decorative panels on display through the arches of Schliemann's House

SCHLIEMANN'S HOUSE ✪

Almost opposite Zonar's *zaharoplasteion* (pastry shop), on the street popularly known as Panepistimiou and officially known as Venizelou, stands the mansion where the discoverer of Troy, Mycenae and much else besides once lived. Designed and built for Heinrich Schliemann by Ernst Ziller, this once-grand mansion housed the Supreme Court of Appeal until recently, but at the time of writing looked rather grimy and forlorn. There are plans to move the Numismatic Collection (➤ 19) here from the National Archaeological Museum after renovation work, but at the moment the rather optimistic sign outside is the only hint of action!

➕ 29D3
✉ Panepistimiou
Ⓜ Syntagma when opened
🚌 23, 25, 230

Did you know ?

In the Panathenaic Games, the victors received commemorative amphoras containing about 40 kilos of olive oil. In the 6th century BC a statesman named Solon introduced laws to protect the olive oil industry. For a time, anyone cutting down an olive tree could be executed. Today, there are about 130 million cultivated olive trees in Greece.

STÁDIO (OLYMPIC STADIUM)
(➤ 26, TOP TEN)

57C1
Entrance to southern
slopes of Acropolis on
Leoforos Dionysiou
Areopagitou

322-4625

Daily 8:30–2:30. Closed
public holidays

230

None

Moderate

Below: *not much remains
of the Theatre of
Dionysos, but the
columns supporting the
stage include some fine
carvings*

THÉATRO DIONÝSOU (THEATRE OF DIONYSOS) ✪✪

Standing below the Acropolis on its southern slopes, this
theatre in its prime held 17,000 people in 64 tiers and was
the venue for an annual drama festival. Here, the citizens
of Athens witnessed the birth of European drama, in the
first theatre ever to be built of stone, where the premières
of plays by Aristophanes, Sophocles and other great
dramatists were performed. Initially the theatre was a
wooden structure, followed by a stone building in 342–26
BC, and finally by the Roman theatre whose remains are
what can be seen today. There are some amusingly
detailed Dionysian statues supporting the stage, and
marble barriers from the times when wild animals fought
in the arena, which was also used for gladiatorial contests.
In the front rows are the marble thrones for visiting digni-
taries. In the rock behind the theatre is a cave which was
once held sacred to the Goddess Artemis, and where a
Byzantine chapel was later built.

28A1
Philopáppou Hill

324-4395

19 May–Sep, nightly at
10:15, extra shows
Wed, Sun 8:15

££

230

None

Expensive

THÉATRO FILOPÁPPOU (PHILOPAPPOU THEATRE) ✪✪

On the western slopes of Philopappou Hill is this theatre,
also known as the Dora Stratou Dance Theatre. Dora
Stratou was a renowned Greek dancer, who preserved
traditional Greek dances, music and costumes, and later
founded her own dance school and dance company, which
performs flamboyant shows here every night throughout
the summer months. To reach the theatre, take the
entrance to the Pnyx which is opposite the Acropolis
entrance on Areopagitou, and follow the signs which direct
you to the far side of the hill.

VIVLIOTHÍKI ADRIANOÚ (LIBRARY OF HADRIAN) ✪

This group of buildings, near the Agora, was built by Emperor Hadrian sometime after AD 132 to house his library, but the building design incorporated a walled courtyard around a central garden and pool. This may sound modest, and today's ruins might suggest that was the case, but it was an extensive building – the largest that Hadrian built in Athens – and the courtyard contained 100 columns. It has unfortunately been closed to the public for some time while thorough excavations are undertaken. When eventually reopened, it should be possible to for visitors to inspect the library, with its recesses for the rolled manuscripts of books.

➕ 56B2
✉ Eolou
Ⓜ Monastiráki

The Byzantine Museum's collection encompasses frescoes, religious artefacts and icons, such as this decaying but still vivid example

VIZANTINÓ MOUSEÍO (BYZANTINE MUSEUM) ✪✪

Another of Athens' specialist collections, this is delightfully housed in an 1840s villa with its own courtyard, filled with flowers and orange trees. The villa was home to the Duchesse de Plaisance, a French widow who had been married to one of Napoleon's generals and who fell in love with Greece and created this Florentine villa in what was then the outskirts of Athens. The bulk of the collection is made up of Byzantine icons, many in glorious reds and golds, and while it is an extensive collection covering 1,500 years of Byzantine Art, it is probably best appreciated by the connoisseur, particularly as the labelling is limited and mainly in Greek. There are also bibles, statues, embroidery and mosaics, and in the building at the far end of the museum grounds is the reconstruction of an early Christian basilica and a complete, re-created Byzantine church.

➕ 29E2
✉ Vasilissis Sofias 22
☎ 723-1570, 711-1027
🕐 Tue–Sun 8:30–3. Closed public holidays
🚌 234
♿ None
💰 Moderate

In the Know

If you only have a short time to visit Athens, or would like to get a real flavour of the city, here are some ideas:

Relaxing in a doorway, as good a place as any

10
Ways to Be a Local

Slow down. Athens is fast, busy and noisy, but Athenians always find ways of relaxing.

Visit the markets, whether you buy or merely browse.

Take a siesta. Athens wakes early and parties till late, but recuperates from about 2–5PM: an even better idea in the hot summer months.

Stroll in the Pláka in the early evening.

Eat late, or you may be eating alone.

Sing or dance, preferably in a place where you're the only tourist in sight.

Drink moderately. Greeks know how to enjoy themselves, but you will seldom see drunken bad behaviour.

Dress appropriately and cover up when visiting churches and monasteries.

Don't compliment Turkey, or call Greek coffee Turkish coffee.

Don't scold children. Greeks have great patience with even the most fractious of children.

10
Good Places to Have Lunch

Aerides (£) If it's cool go upstairs and gaze at the Tower of the Winds. If sunny, there are plenty of tables outside.
✉ Markou Avriliou 3
☎ 322-6266

Dionysos-Zonar's (£££) You're paying for the view when you eat here, though there are cheaper lunch offerings on the menu. But what a view!
✉ Lykavittós ☎ 722-6374

Dionysos-Zonar's (££) Another branch of this popular chain, but this one too has excellent views, looking across at the Parthenon.
✉ Rovertou Galli 43
☎ 922-1998

Five Brothers (£) Outdoor seating in a quiet street near the Roman Agora.
✉ Eolou 3 ☎ 325-0088

GB Corner (£££) If you can't afford to stay at the Grande Bretagne Hotel, at least savour the atmosphere with a meal here.
✉ Grande Bretagne Hotel, Syntagma Square
☎ 323-8361

Mikrolimano (£££) Innumerable fish tavernas surround this small harbour in busy Piraeus. Excellent but expensive fish. Choose a place that suits your taste and budget.

Palia Athina (££) Just out of the Pláka, and one of the author's favourites for its authentic food.
✉ Nikis 46 ☎ 331-2975

O Platanos (£) There can be few better places to eat in summer than outside here, in a quiet corner beneath a plane tree.
✉ Diogenous 4 ☎ 322-0666

Platanos (£) An old Athens favourite maintains high standards and great atmosphere.
✉ Diogenous 4 ☎ 322-0666

Sigalas (£) Bustling old taverna in the heart of Athens, not for gourmets but as Greek as it gets.
✉ Monastiráki 2
☎ 321-3036

10
Top Activities

Golf: there's an international course at Glyfada, on the coast just beyond the airport ☎ 894-6820.

Horse-riding: there are a few clubs around Athens. Contact the Hellenic Riding Club, Paradisou 18 ☎ 682-6128.

Jogging: contact the Hash House Harriers Jogging Club in Kifissia to join locals and ex-pats for a run ☎ 621-9821.

Marathon: if you want to run a marathon then you may as well cover the original route, from Marathon to Athens. This is done twice a year; details from SEGAS, Syngrou 137 ☎ 935-9302.

Sailing: there are marinas, yachting and sailing clubs in Piraeus, Glyfada, Vouliagmeni and other suburbs of Athens. Information from the Hellenic Yachting Federation, Akti Navarchou Kountouridti 7 in Piraeus ☎ 413-7351.

Sea Fishing: with the Aegean on its doorstep, there are plenty of opportunities. Contact the Harbour Master's Office in Piraeus, ☎ 451-

1131, or the Anglers and Maritime Sports Club at Akti Moutsopoulou, also in Piraeus ☎ 451-5731.

Swimming: best beaches are at Glyfada, but they suffer from airport noise, though this doesn't deter the Athenians. Otherwise pay to use a hotel pool, such as the Hilton.

Tennis: very popular, with courts all over the city. Try the Athens Tennis Club at Vasilissis Olgas 2 ☎ 923-2872.

Walking: with a shortage of taxis and packed public transport, you are advised to walk in Athens, and a climb up Lykabettos Hill will definitely get you fit!

Water-skiing: for opportunities within reach of Athens contact the Water-skiing Club at Sturnara 32 ☎ 523-1875.

5
Specialist Museums

- **Greek Historical Costume Museum**, ⊠ Dimokritou 7 ☎ 362-9513
- **Philatelic Museum**, ⊠ Fokianou 2 ☎ 751-9066
- **Cinema Museum**, ⊠ Kriezotou 3 ☎ 362-6266
- **Venizelos Museum**, ⊠ Vasilissis Sofias, behind the statue of Venizelos ☎ 941-2393
- **International Museum of Shellfish**, ⊠ Pindou 14 ☎ 941-2393

5
Greek Dishes to Try

- *Kalamaris* or *kalamarakia*: fried baby squid
- *Saganaki*: deep-fried cheese
- *Spedzofai*: spicy stew of sausage, pepper, tomatoes
- *Vriam*: ratatouille-type dish of fresh vegetables
- *Yemista*: stuffed tomatoes and/or peppers

10
Ways to Avoid a Greek Salad

Try one of Athens's many non-Greek restaurants:
- Japanese: Michiko (➤ 94)
- Chinese: Golden Flower (➤ 93)
- Polynesian: Kona Kai (➤ 94)
- French: Prunier (➤ 95)
- Italian: Boschetto (➤ 92)
- Korean: Far East (➤ 93)
- Armenian: Tria Asteria, Melitos 7 ☎ 935-8134
- Spanish: Ispanika Gonia, Theayenous 22 ☎ 723-1393
- Czech: Bohemia, Dhimou Tseliou ☎ 642-6341
- Mexican: Blue Velvet, Ermou 116 ☎ 323-9047

Sunset, and the perfect time for some solitude and a spot of sea fishing in the peaceful waters

Excursions

If you are only making a weekend visit to Athens you may want to limit yourself to the city itself, though an evening bus ride to romantic Cape Sounion (► 76) is easily done, and Piraeus (► 86) and Kifissia (► 81) are on the metro. With a few more days, though, there are many other exciting options, available as one- or two-day tours through hotels and travel agents; alternatively, most are equally easy to arrange for yourself.

Those who have never visited a Greek island should certainly take the opportunity. The nearest major island, Aegina (► 75), is only 40 minutes away by Flying Dolphin. Athens is also the hub of the excellent Greek bus network, with cheap and regular services to famous places such as Mycenae (► 83), Epidavros (► 80) and the incomparable Delphi (► 78).

> *'Delphi, I should think perhaps the Greekest thing of all. It comes nearest to being serious, and is charming...'*
>
> HENRY ADAMS
> *Letter to Elizabeth Cameron*
> (1898)

———————— • ————————

Rounding the Cape: a view of Sounion from the sea shows that its temple is splendid from every angle

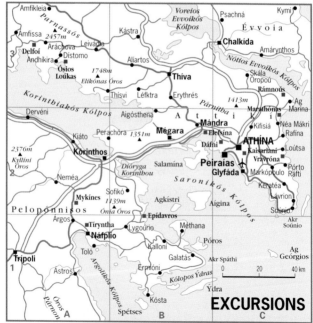

EXCURSIONS

Amfikleia
Parnassós
Voreios Evvoïkós Kólpos
Psachná
Kymi
Amfissa
2457m
Aráchova
Leivádia
Kástra
Évvoia
Chalkida
Amárynthos
Delfoí
Andhíkira
Dístomo
Aliartos
Thíva
Nótios Evvoïkós Kólpos
Ósios Loúkas
1748m
Elikónas Óros
Skála Oropoú
Korinthiakós Kólpos
Thísvi
Léfktra
Erythrés
Rámnoús
Párnitha
1413m
Ag Marína
Dervéni
Aigósthena
Attikí
Marathónas
Kiáto
Perachóra
1351m
Mégara
Mándra
Eléfsina
Kifisiá
Néa Mákri
Rafína
Korinthos
2376m
Kyllíni Óros
Dáfni
ATHÍNA
Kaisarianí
Loútsa
Neméa
Dióryga Korínthou
Salamína
Peiraías
Glyfáda
Vravróna
Markópoulo
Pórto Ráfti
Mykínes
Sofikó
1139m
Ónia Óros
Agkístri
Aígina
Saronikós Kólpos
Keratéa
Lávrion
Pelopónnisos
Árgos
Tíryntha
Epídavros
Lygoúrio
Méthana
Akr Soúnio
Soúnio
Náfplio
Póros
Ag Geórgios
Tripoli
Toló
Kallóni
Galatás
Akr Spáthi
0   20   40 km
Ástros
Ermióni
Kólopos Ýdras
Óros Párnon
Kósta
Spétses
Ydra

74

AÍGINA (AEGINA) ★★

Being so close to Athens, Aegina is a popular weekend retreat for Athenians so it can be very busy, especially in high summer. In addition to its proximity, it owes its popularity to the fact that it is quite a green island, with some good beaches, and an exceptional temple – the **Temple of Aphaia**, which was built in about 490 BC and is regarded as one of the best-preserved Doric temples in Greece.

The temple is easy to reach as there are regular buses from Aegina Town, while a visit booked through a travel agent will certainly include a trip to it. The temple is about 60 years older than the Parthenon, and equally impressively set, on a pine-covered hill. If visibility is good and you have binoculars, you can see the Acropolis (► 17) from here, as well as the Temple of Poseidon at Cape Sounion (► 76).

Near by is the bustling port and resort of Agía Marina. If you especially want to visit the temple some of the ferries from Piraeus stop here, as well as at Aegina Town, so check first. Agía Marina is a busy package holiday resort, and the island's capital, Aegina Town, has far more of an authentic Greek feel to it. There are some fine old buildings dating from the time when this was the capital of Greece (1826–8), after the War of Independence. The resort also features some interesting churches, the house where the novelist, poet and dramatist Nikos Kazantzakis (1883–1957) wrote *Zorba the Greek*, a small museum, and good waterfront fish tavernas.

✚ 74B2

🍴 Cafés/restaurants (£) in Agía Marina

🚌 Bus from Aegina Town to Agía Marina stops at the temple

Temple of Aphaia

✉ 0297-32398

🕐 Temple: Mon–Fri 8:30–7, Sat–Sun 8:30–3; site museum open daily 8:30–1. Both closed public holidays

♿ Few: phone first

💰 Expensive

Yachts in the harbour at Aegina show that Greece is still very much a maritime nation

---

Did you know ?

In Greek mythology the inhabitants of Aegina were the Myrmidons. The name came about after the original inhabitants were destroyed in a plague by Hera, wife of Zeus, jealous of her husband's love for Aegina, who gave the island its name.
Zeus repopulated the island after a plea by Aeacus, grandfather of Achilles, and because Aeacus had been inspired by the sight of an anthill, and asked for an equally numerous population, the new inhabitants of Aegina became the Myrmidons (the Greek for ants is myrmekes*).*

Daily 10–sunset. Closed
public holidays

Restaurants nearby (££)

Sounion bus, no
number, leaves from
Mavromateon terminal

None

Moderate

*Cape Sounion, with its
Temple of Poseidon, was
known to Homer and the
ancient Greeks as 'the
sacred cape'*

ÁKRA SOÚNIO (CAPE SOUNION) ✪✪✪

The most dramatic way to see Cape Sounion for the first
time is from the Athens coastal road: turn a bend and
suddenly, in the distance, the magnificent white ruins of
the Temple of Poseidon can be seen standing proudly at
the tip of the cape on top of the 60m high headland. In
actuality, when you get close, you see that the marble is
grey (it was mined only 5km away at Agrileza).

It is easy to get to and from the Cape by bus from
central Athens, and a popular time to make the journey is
in the late afternoon or early evening, in order to be there
for the sunset. A spectacular sunset is not guaranteed, but
they are frequent and there can be few more splendid
sights than to watch the temple turning into a silhouette
against the red sky over the Aegean. The large island due
west is Aegina (➤ 75), and beyond that is the east coast
of the Peloponnese. To the east is Kea, the closest of the
Cycladic Islands.

The temple was built in 444 BC on the foundations of
another building which has been dated back to 490 BC. The
temple originally had 34 columns, but only 15 remain
standing today. One of these bears the scratched initials of
the English poet and Grecophile, Lord Byron (➤ 14), who
visited here in 1810, though the temple is now roped off
to help preserve it from any modern-day attempts at
adding graffiti.

76

Attica:
A Drive Through History

If flying to Athens and hiring a car, start the trip by heading east through Attikí (Attica).

No matter which terminal you fly into, head east towards Cape Sounion (➤ 76). It quickly becomes a delightful drive along the coast of the Saronic Gulf.

The Temple of Poseidon is unmistakable on its headland, at the southern tip of Attica. There are hotels here for those wanting to break the journey.

Continue north from Soúnio on the main road towards Markópoulo.

Markópoulo is a pleasant place to pause. There are cafés and, in a walled garden, two chapels worth seeing: Ágia Paraskevi and Ágia Thekla.

In Markópoulo leave the main road to Athens, and take the smaller road towards Pórto Ráfti.

Pórto Ráfti is an attractive beach resort and small port, set in a large bay: a good spot for a meal of fresh fish.

From Pórto Ráfti take the coast road to Vravróna, looking for signs for the site and museum of ancient Vravróna (Brauron ➤ 90). From Vavróna keep on the coast road into Rafína, another lively port resort. Leave Rafína on the Athens road (54) but turn right towards Néa Mákri and Marathonas (route 83).

The memorial mound at Marathónas (Marathon ➤ 83) is on the right, after Néa Mákri. Here 10,000 Athenians defeated 30,000 invading Persians. The 192 Athenian casualties are buried beneath the mound.

Continue towards Marathon but before reaching it look for the right turn to Ágia Marina and Rámnoús.

The remote site at Rámnoús (➤ 88) is at the very end of the road, short on ruins but full of atmosphere. A world away from Athens and airports.

Distance
130km

Time
3 hours, excluding long breaks

Start point
✚ 74C2
Any of the Athens airport terminals.
Add at least 30 minutes if starting from central Athens.

End point
✚ 74C3
Rámnoús

Lunch
Xanolia Taverna (£)
✚ Vravróna
✉ 0294-71020

A fisherman at Rafína tries to catch his own lunch: visitors can rely on the port's excellent seafood restaurants

74C2
581-1558
Daily 8:30–3. Closed
public holidays
A16 from Plateía
Eleftherías, Monstiráki
None
Moderate

DÁFNÍ (DAPHNI) ✪

Some of the finest Byzantine mosaics in the whole of Greece can be found in this 11th-century monastery, close by the thundering noise of the main Athens–Corinth highway. The glorious golden mosaic of Christ Pantocrator stares down from the dome of the church, and below this are mosaics of the Annunciation, Nativity, Baptism and Transfiguration. The buildings themselves are also well preserved, on the site of what was once a Temple of Apollo. One of Apollo's symbols was the laurel – or *daphni*, in Greek.

74A3
Site and museum:
0265-82312
Site Mon–Fri 7:30–6:30,
Sat–Sun 8:30–3;
museum Mon 12–6:30,
Tue–Fri 7:30–7:30,
Sat–Sun 8:30–3
In village of Delphi
Daily, from Liossion 260
terminal
None
Expensive; free Sun

*The Sacred Way at Delphi
leads past the Treasury,
probably built to celebrate
victory at Marathon*

DELFOÍ (DELPHI) ✪✪✪

The ancient Greeks thought Delphi the centre of the world, and anyone visiting the site today will understand why. It has an indisputable atmosphere and an impressive setting between high cliffs and a vast valley of olive trees which falls away below you.

Pilgrims visited the Oracles at Delphi from roughly the 12th century BC to the 4th century AD, to seek advice on all kinds of subjects. The most famous of all the Oracles was the Sibyl, whose rock can still be seen today at the side of the Sacred Way which winds from the entrance up to the remains of the Temple of Apollo.

The temple ruins date from the 4th century BC, as does the 5,000-seat theatre behind. Climb to the top row of the theatre for one of the best views over the site and down the valley. Above here is a well-preserved stadium and near by is also a superb museum.

Delfoí Drive: to the Centre of the World

The Ancient Greeks thought that Delphi was the centre of the world, and when you drive to it through the Parnassos Mountains, you may understand why.

From central Athens look for signs to Lamia, Thessaloniki and the E75 National Highway.

Thessaloniki, Greece's second city, is well worth a visit for its Roman remains, museums, Macedonian culture and lively sea-front eating places.

Stay on the E75 for about 85km until you reach the turn-off for Thíva (Thebes) which you take.

The name of Thebes resonates with history, but the present-day town is mainly notable for its excellent museum.

As you skirt around Thebes, follow the road signs for Leivádia, which is about another 50km further on from Thebes.

Leivádia is a far more attractive place to stop than Thebes, with some ancient remains and a lovely setting on the banks of the River Herkina.

Whether you divert into Leivádia or not, you will now pick up the signs for Delphi, as the road climbs up into the mountains.

One diversion you must make if time allows is to take the left turn to Dístomo, some 20km after Leivádia. Beyond Dístomo is the remote Monastery of Ossios Loukas, one of the finest in all Greece and renowned for its frescoes.

Continuing past the Dístomo turning, this main road leads you all the way to Delphi, first passing through the delightful mountain town of Aráchova.

Stop off in Aráchova for lunch and a walk round, before proceeding the last few kilometres to Delphi.

Distance
180km

Time
2 hours, excluding long breaks

Start point
✚ 74C2
Central Athens

End point
✚ 74A3

Lunch
Karathanassi (£)
✚ Delphon 56, Aráchova
✉ 0267-31360

Side streets in Aráchova invite exploration: some lead to paths which go up into the Parnassos Mountains

The audience gathers for an evening performance at Epidavros, whose circular stage is unusual for Greek theatres

74B2
Gioga/Iera 1
554-6019
Tue–Sun 8–3. Closed public holidays
A16
None
Moderate

ELEFSÍNA (ELEUSIS) ✪

The Sacred Way from Athens to Eleusis is scarcely sacred today, with a multi-lane motorway running past dockyards, factories and oil refineries. But in the 6th century BC, this was one of the most sacred sites in the ancient world, home to a cult which attracted up to 30,000 followers. Their rituals were so secret that no records remain – only speculation. Speculation will also be needed to imagine the site as it was, for these days only foundations and overgrown pathways remain, though models in the museum help the visitor build up a picture.

74B1
Site and museum 0753-22009
Site daily 8–6; museum Mon 12–6, Tue–Sun 8–6 (winter), 7:30–7:30 (summer). Closed public holidays
Daily from Kifissou 100 terminal
None
Expensive; free Sun in winter

EPÍDAVROS (EPIDAVROS) ✪✪✪

The ancient theatre at Epidavros is the finest in Greece, for its setting, its state of preservation and its acoustics. It is said that you can hear a pin drop on the stage from the top of the 55 rows of seats.

The theatre was built in the 4th century BC but only discovered at the end of the 19th century. It was finally restored in 1954. It can seat 14,000 and is still in use for an annual drama festival held in July and August.

Spectators look out over the site of Epidavros, which was dedicated to the healing God Asklepios, the son of Apollo. The site has the remains of a guesthouse, bath, gymnasium and sanctuary buildings, although many are overgrown. The site museum contains a good collection of statues, including some of Asklepios, and a partial reconstruction of the Tholos or rotunda.

Did you know ?

The idea for a canal across the narrow isthmus at Corinth was first put forward by Emperor Nero in AD 67. He is said to have started the digging with a golden shovel before leaving 6,000 Jewish prisoners to complete the work. However, the canal was only finished in 1893, having taken a French engineering company 12 years to construct.

KAISARIANÍ ✪

The main water supply for Athens once came from the spring here, which was known as the Imperial (*kaisariane*) Spring after Emperor Hadrian, who built the aqueduct to convey water to the city. The cluster of beautifully preserved monastery buildings stands 450m up on the slopes of Mount Hymettus, with cells, refectory and kitchen among those remaining. Twelfth-century frescoes are among the many attractions of this quiet retreat, just a few kilometres outside Athens.

74C2
723-6619
Tue–Sun 8:30–3. Closed public holidays
234
None
Cheap

KIFISIÁ (KIFISSIA) ✪✪

This fashionable suburb at the northern end of the metro line has long been an enviable address in Athens. At 276m, its cooler climate attracts the wealthier citizens, as a glance at the high-street shops will indicate. The town is an attractive and easy day out for the visitor too, though not all north-bound trains go all the way to Kifissia, so check the destination board first. Those that do pass the modern Olympic stadium at Irini. From the Kifissia stop you can hail one of the horse-drawn carriages for a tour around the area, with its many grand mansions. Alternatively, simply walk up through the park, cross the busy road and continue on up, perhaps pausing on the left at Varsos, said to be the oldest of Athens' many *zaharoplasteions* (pastry shops). A left turn at the next junction takes you to the Goulandris Natural History Museum, a small but impressive collection, which naturally concentrates on the flora and fauna of Greece. It is especially good on birds, butterflies, sea shells, and environmental problems. The herbarium alone is said to contain over 250,000 specimens.

74C2
Goulandris Natural History Museum, Levidou 13
808-6405
Sat and Sun 9–2. Currently closed weekdays, public holidays
Café (£)
Kifissia
None
Moderate

Solid columns stand in the Roman Agora of Ancient Corinth

➕ 74A2
☎ Site and museum:
0741-31207
🕓 Daily 8–7 (winter 8–6).
Closed public holidays
♿ None
💰 Expensive

KÓRINTHOS (CORINTH) ⭐⭐

It is a pity that the modern town of Kórinthos is not more appealing, for on its doorstep the visitor can see the site of Ancient Corinth, the looming hilltop ruins of Acrocorinth and one of the wonders of the modern world – the Corinth Canal. It is true that the last of these will not detain you long, but it should not be missed, for it is a beautiful, as well as a brilliant, engineering achievement. It is almost 6.5km long and 90m high but only 27m across, making it unsuitable for many of today's supertankers.

Acrocorinth was also a startling engineering feat in its day. This ancient acropolis has walls that run for 2km on top of the hill which dominates the surrounding plain and the Gulf of Corinth. Inside the walls are the remains of further fortifications, houses, mosques and churches, and the views from here are extraordinary.

Down below is the site of Ancient Corinth, once the Roman capital of Greece, with a population of 300,000, supported by a further 460,000 slaves. It also had a great reputation for licentious living, so St Paul's Epistles to the Corinthians were particularly relevant. The well-preserved remains and the Archaeological Museum on the site help the visitor to visualise the city as it was (apart from the bawdy behaviour). The most noticeable building here is the Temple of Apollo, which dates from the 6th century BC, making it one of the oldest of the many temples to be found in Greece.

MARATHÓNAS (MARATHON) ★

In 490 BC news of the Greek victory over the Persians at Marathon was relayed to Athens by a soldier called Pheidippides, who ran the 41km to deliver his message and then died. The event is commemorated in the name of today's marathon race, and the battle is commemorated in the mound under which the 192 Athenians who lost their lives in the fight were buried. The fact that 6,400 Persians are also said to have been killed gives the scale of the heroic victory. There is a small museum near to the modern village of Marathon, an otherwise fairly nondescript place, and above the museum a hill which gives a good view of the Plain of Marathon, once filled with those warring soldiers.

➕ 74C2
☎ 0294-55155 for tomb and Archaeological Museum
🕐 Both Tue–Sun 8:30–3. Closed public holidays
🚌 Marathónas bus, no number, from Mavromateon terminal (1¼ hours)
♿ None

MYKÍNES (MYCENAE) ★★★

'I have gazed upon the face of Agamemnon,' claimed German archaeologist Heinrich Schliemann to the King of Greece when he unearthed a golden mask on this site. This and other stunning golden treasures are on display in the National Archaeological Museum in Athens (▶ 18–19). Agamemnon's palace or not – and later carbon-dating suggests not – the ruins are still among the most famous and popular in Greece. Few visitors will not experience a thrill when seeing for the first time the famous Lion Gate (c1250 BC), almost as familiar an image of Greece as the Parthenon. Beyond the Gate, on the right, is the Royal Cemetery where the golden treasures were found. Near by is the Treasury of Atreus, a simple but superbly striking royal burial tomb.

➕ 74A2
☎ 0751-76585
🕐 Daily 8–7 (winter 8–5). Closed public holidays
🚌 Take Náfplio bus and ask for Mycenae
♿ None
💰 Expensive

When entering the Lion Gate at Mycenae, look up at the lintel to see the pivots for the wooden door which was originally here

74A1

Café, restaurants
(£–£££) in town

Daily from Kifissou, 100
terminal

Archaeological Museum

Plateia Syntagmatos

0752-27502

Tue–Sun, 8:30–3.
Closed public holidays

None

Moderate

Folklore Museum

Vasilissis Alexandrou 1

0752-28379

Closed until 1999 so
check

War Museum

Leoforos Amalias

0752-25591

Tue–Sun, 9–2. Closed
public holidays

None

Free

*Colourful window
displays adorn the houses
of Náfplio*

NÁFPLIO ✪✪✪

Náfplio is far from being the largest place in the Peloponnese – that distinction goes to the port of Pátra, Greece's third largest city – but it is certainly one of the most attractive. Indeed, many Greeks regard it as the prettiest town in the whole of Greece.

There are several reasons for its charm. It looks like a Greek island port, clustered at the base of a headland dominated by not one but two fortresses. Its streets are old and narrow, with Italianate balconies which are flower-filled in summer. It has an immensely attractive large, open, traffic-free main square, while across its attractive harbour can be seen the mountain peaks of the rest of the Peloponnese.

Náfplio is also very cosmopolitan for a small town, attracting artists and craftsmen, and with the daily papers of the world available in several of its shops. It has a range of very good eating places, a small beach and easy access to important ancient sites such as Mycenae, Tiryns and Epídavros. It also has a unique place in Greece's modern history, for it was Náfplio, not Athens, which was the first capital of modern Greece. The country's first President, Kapodistrias, lived and was assassinated here.

Its history is reflected in the two main fortresses, a **war museum**, **folklore museum** and an **archaeological museum** with some fascinating items. Little wonder that Náfplio is such a popular spot for Athenians who want a holiday, or simply a short break from the city – it is a mere two hours' drive away.

To Greece's Old Capital at Náfplio

Náfplio was the capital of Greece from 1829 to 1834 and is one of the most attractive towns on the mainland.

Leave Athens following the signs for Kórinthos (Corinth), which takes you out of the city past Daphni (➤ 78) and Eleusis (➤ 80) and on to the National Highway, the E94.

This is a beautiful coastal run once the industrial outskirts have been left behind. The island of Salamis (➤ 88) can be seen just off the coast.

Continue on the E94 all the way to the Corinth Canal (➤ 82), but watch out for the bridge going over the canal as you can be across it before you're aware of what you're crossing.

Pull up at the cafés and shops on the near side of the bridge, and walk out across it to get the best look at this marvel of engineering.

About 8km beyond the canal look for the left turn off the main highway marked Argos.

This road passes the archaeological site of Mycenae (➤ 83), and if you only have one diversion on your drive to Náfplio, make it this one. Look for the turning off to the left, which is signposted. The site is only a short way off the main road.

Continue towards Argos, and when there follow the signs for Náfplio.

The road passes another archaeological site, off the road to the left at Tíryntha (Tiryns), much quieter than Mycenae but a dramatic setting.

Continue on into Náfplio (➤ 84).

Distance
150km

Time
2 hours, excluding long breaks

Start point
🞤 74C2
Central Athens

End point
🞤 74A1
Náfplio

Lunch
Kakanarakis (£)
✉ Vasilissis Olgas 18, Nafplion
☎ 0752-25371

The Corinth Canal shortened the sea journey from Italy to Athens by over 320km

Archaeological Museum

- 74C2
- Harilaou Trikoupi 31
- 452-1598
- Tue–Sun 8:30–3. Closed public holidays
- Piraeus
- None
- Moderate

Naval Museum

- 74C2
- Akti Themistokleous
- 451-6264
- Tue–Sat 9–2. Closed public holidays
- Piraeus
- None
- Cheap

PEIRAÍAS (PIRAEUS)

Piraeus is easily accessible from central Athens, being at the end of the Metro line, though its charms are limited. Imagine the traffic of Athens and then add the bustle of one of the Mediterranean's busiest ports. Nevertheless, it can be worth a trip out on a Sunday morning when the flea-market operates in the streets behind the metro/railway station. It is part of the street life that recalls the award-winning 1959 film, *Never on Sunday*, starring Melina Mercouri (➤ 14) as a Piraeus prostitute with the proverbial heart of gold.

It was near the magnificent cathedral of Ágia Triadha, on Filonos, behind the Town Hall, that workmen in 1959 found the impressive bronze statues which form the principal reason for visiting Piraeus's **Archaeological Museum**. The exhibits in the first hall were found in 1930–1 in a sunken ship that had been bound for Italy and which was discovered in Piraeus harbour.

Turn left out of the museum entrance and walk straight down the main street to the Limin Zeas harbour. Turn right here and a short way along the front, across the street, is the **Naval Museum** of Greece. This includes model ships, from ancient triremes to modern-day battleships, and displays covering some of the great naval battles in Greek waters, such as the Battle of Salamis, along with numerous documents and drawings, letters and relics.

The Mikrolimano harbour in Piraeus is also the place where Athenians go to find the best fish tavernas for a leisurely summer Sunday lunch or evening meal.

Piraeus is a sprawling port with two small harbours and one very large one. If you're not familiar with it and you plan to visit an island, it is vital to check in advance, on a map, where your boat leaves from, and how best to get there. For the Argo-Saronic islands mentioned in this guide, ferries leave from Akti Possidhonios and further round the same quay along Akti Miaouli. Hydrofoils going direct to Aegina leave from close by on Akti Tselepi, but hydrofoils for the other Argo-Saronic islands all leave from the Zea Marina harbour.

A ship in the harbour at Piraeus gets its name spruced up for the new season

PÓROS ✪✪

A visit to Póros gets you two islands for the price of one. Two separate small islands are joined by a causeway. You are also just 400m from the mainland across the passage or ford (*póros*) that gives the island its name. Only an hour from Athens, Póros naturally gets as busy as the other Argo-Saronic islands. For a lovely escape, cross to the mainland and walk to the lemon groves of Limonodhassos, where 30,000 trees perfume the air and paths meander through the groves up to a small taverna serving fresh lemon juice.

Back in Póros Town it's also possible to meander through some of its narrow back streets, to visit the town's small Archaeological Museum, or sit in the water-front cafés and tavernas watching boats and people come and go. Some quite large boats dock in Póros, and as the town's houses tumble right down to the waterfront, it is strange to see people on deck at the same level as some of the houses. In the interior of the island you can see the scant remains of a 6th-century Temple to Poseidon, but Póros is more a place for enjoying modern holiday life than for the ancient past.

RAFÍNA ✪

This port, a 40-minute bus ride from Athens, is the departure point for many of the ferries to the northeast Aegean islands, to some of the Cyclades and the Dodecanese, and to Evvia. It is also renowned for the quality of its seafood restaurants, clustered round the small fishing harbour, and a trip out here for lunch can make a wonderful break from the big city.

✚ 74B1
✉ Tourist Police: on the waterfront
☎ Tourist Police: 0298-22462
🎫 Daily May–Sep
🍴 Many cafés and restaurants (£–£££)

The houses of Póros tumble down almost into the harbour

✚ 74C2
🍴 Many (££–£££)
🚌 From Mavromateon bus station in Athens

Distant views of the few ruins of the Temple of Themis in Rámnoús

➕ 74C3
☎ 0294-63477
🕐 Mon–Sat 7–6, Sun 8–6. Closed public holidays
🚌 Rámnoús/Ag. Marina bus, no number, from Mavromateon terminal
♿ None
💰 Moderate

➕ 74B2
🍴 Several in Salamina town, Selina and Eandio (£)

RÁMNOÚS ✪

This is one of the remotest classical sites that is actually accessible from Athens, though it is awkward to reach unless you have a car. For that reason you may well have the site to yourself, especially out of season. It was sacred to two goddesses, Themis (Goddess of Justice) and Nemesis (mother of Helen of Troy), but little remains of their two temples, the foundations of which are scattered and overgrown. Nature has largely taken over, and that is part of its charm. It is a place for imagination, peace, wildlife and a picnic.

SALAMÍNA (SALAMIS) ✪

Salamis is something of an oddity. It is actually the largest of the Argo-Saronic islands but probably the least known outside Greece because it is the least developed for tourism. In fact the capital, Salamis Town, doesn't even have a hotel. It is only a kilometre from Piraeus, making it a very short hop on the ferry, and indeed many Athenians commute to work from here. It was the birthplace of Euripides and its name is best known as the setting for the Battle of Salamis, in 480 BC, when the large Persian fleet was defeated by the much smaller but speedier fleet of Greek triremes.

Salamis Town has little to recommend it, and the port where the ferries arrive even less, the two being 3km apart and connected by a bus service. However, if you can devote a little time to exploration, the island has its attractions: the fishing harbour and old mansions at Ágios Nikolaos, the 17th-century Monastery of Faneromeni and the small resort of Peristeria are all worth a visit.

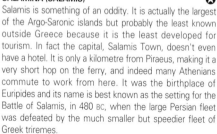

An elderly and obliging resident of Spétses

SPÉTSES ✪✪

Spétses is the Argo-Saronic island furthest from Athens, but it can still be reached in little over two hours on one of the fast Flying Dolphin services. It's less expensive than Hydra, has better beaches than Póros or Hydra, is relatively green (its name is a corruption of the Greek word for 'piney') and therefore is just as popular as all the other islands, despite the distance involved!

74B1
Tourist Police: Botassi
Tourist Police: 0298-73100
Museum Tue–Sun 8:30–2:30
Many (££–£££)
Museum: moderate

Spétses became renowned in the late 1960s as the setting for the cult novel by British author John Fowles, *The Magus*, which was later filmed. Fowles lived and taught here and renamed it Phraxos for the purposes of his fiction. The factual Spétses town has, like Hydra Town, many handsome 18th-century mansions built on the strength of its wealthy merchant shipping fleets. One of the finest, built in 1795, now houses the island's museum and is well worth a visit. Spétses' charm as a place to visit, or to stay overnight on a jaunt from Athens, is enhanced by a partial ban on cars and a good reputation for eating places.

VRAVRÓNA (BRAURON)

The ancient site and the museum of Brauron are about 15 minutes' walk apart, on the edge of the village of the same name. The site was a centre for the cult of Artemis, goddess of fertility, and there are remains of a 5th-century BC temple dedicated to her, on the site of an even earlier building. A reconstructed scale model of the temple stands in the pleasant museum near by, alongside other finds from the area.

ÝDRA (HYDRA)

If you only have time to visit one Greek island while staying in Athens, there are reasons both for and against choosing Hydra. It takes only a little over 90 minutes to reach on the Flying Dolphin, and when you arrive the harbour looks so extraordinarily beautiful that you will see at once why people fall in love with the Greek islands. On the other hand, a great many people have already fallen in love with Hydra so it can be extremely crowded. It is also not a typically Greek island – but then every island is different, which is part of their charm.

Hydra was colonised by a crowd of Bohemian artists in the 1960s, and became a very fashionable place to live and to visit, with more than a touch of St Tropez about it. Many of the old mansions which line the harbour were sensitively renovated, returning them to the glory of the days when Hydra had a large merchant shipping fleet that created its 18th-century wealth. Today, very strict building controls and a ban on cars ensure that Hydra retains its beauty, though there are, of course, constant commercial pressures to ease the restrictions.

You can escape the crowds and fashionable boutiques by walking to one of the island's fishing villages, or heading up above the town for an hour or so to the convent of Ágia Efpraxia and neighbouring monastery of Profitis Ilias, all a welcome return to a more traditional Greek island life.

74C2

Site and museum 0299-27020

Both Tue–Sun 8:30–3. Closed public holidays

None

304 to Artemi then 2km walk

None

Moderate

74B1

Tourist Police: Votsi, Hydra Town

Tourist Police: 0298-52205

Daily 9AM–10PM, May–Oct

Many cafés and restaurants (£–£££)

Sunlight over the rooftops of Hydra

Where To...

Above: *a taverna in the Pláka area*
Right: *imposing statues of ancient gods abound in Athens*

Athens

Prices

Approximate prices for a three-course meal for one person, without drinks or service:

£ = under 5000dr
££ = 5000–10,000dr
£££ = over 10,000dr

Informality

Athens is a very informal city, and not even the smartest restaurants operate a 'collar and tie' policy. That said, many of the places described as foreign or smart attract people who have dressed up for a special meal, so you may feel a little out of place if you haven't done the same. In cheaper tavernas you will be welcome no matter what you are wearing.

Al Convento (££)

This is one of the more affordable of Athens' several Italian restaurants, and claims to be the oldest. It's a very friendly place serving spaghetti dishes and pizzas, and its house special: pasta and *scaloppini*.

✉ Anapiron Polimou 4–6 ☎ 723-9163 🕓 Mon–Sat dinner 🚇 Syntagma when opened

Bajazzo (£££)

This is arguably the best restaurant in Athens, with prices to match. The inventive ever-changing menu may include beef fillets and *foie gras* in a cognac-cream sauce, or sea-bass in ouzo.

✉ Anapafseos 14 ☎ 921-3013 🕓 Mon–Sat 8PM–3AM, occasional lunches (ring first) 🚌 2, 4, 11, 12

Bakalarakia (£)

Here you'll find simple but good Greek food in what claims to be the oldest taverna in Athens, established in 1865. Salted cod in garlic is the speciality which gives this basement place its name.

✉ Kydathinaion 41 ☎ 322-5084 🕓 Daily 7–12. Closed midsummer 🚇 Monastiráki

Barba Yannis (£)

This great favourite in a student area frequently has queues outside the door. There is impromptu music (not always), brisk service, and a limited menu of good Greek dishes. You won't find a better atmosphere.

✉ Emmanuel Benaki 94 ☎ 330-0185 🕓 Mon–Sat noon–late, Sun lunch. Closed August 🚇 Omonia

Boschetto (£££)

This delightful Italian place is in Evangelismos Park on the edge of Kolonáki and serves fashionable food and fresh pasta, using ingredients popular in both Greece and Italy: squid, spinach, courgettes and cheese.

✉ Alsos Evanelismos ☎ 721-0893 🕓 Mon–Sat, lunch, dinner. Closed lunch in winter, two weeks in August 🚌 234

Chai Long (££)

In a quiet Pláka side street, this attractive Chinese place specialises in Hong Kong recipes and has an extensive menu with set-price options. Good, courteous service.

✉ Mnisikleous 7 ☎ 331-4323 🕓 Daily lunch, dinner. Closed Tue 🚇 Monastiráki

Costoyannis (££)

Situated near the Archaeological Museum is this taverna of great character, appealing to everyone: students, businessmen, tourists. It has a good reputation for appetisers and fish dishes, and a better-than-average house wine.

✉ Zaimi 37 ☎ 821-2496 🕓 Mon–Sat dinner 🚇 Omonia

Da Walter (££)

The Da Walter is a smart Italian place in a smart Kolonáki neighbourhood, offering a more ambitious menu than the simple pizza and pasta places. Try veal in a cognac and mustard sauce, for example. The restaurant has typical, friendly Italian service.

✉ Evzonon 7 ☎ 724-8726 🕓 Daily dinner 🚇 Syntagma when opened

Eden (£)
This eatery serves hearty vegetarian food mingling Greek dishes with slight Middle Eastern influences. You'll also find the tastiest bread in Athens, good coffee with endless refills and – rare in Greece – a non-smoking section.
✉ Lysiou 12 ☎ 324-8858
🕐 Wed–Mon 12–12
🚇 Monastiráki

Ermou and Asomaton (£££)
This stylish restaurant offers an extensive menu of sophisticated Greek and international dishes, including vegetarian and unusual options: smoked eel or chicken in yoghurt, mint, mustard and lemon.
✉ Ermou 137 ☎ 324-6337
🕐 Mon–Fri 8PM–2AM, Sat–Sun 11–5, 8–2 🚇 Theseion

Famagusta (££)
Many Greek restaurants overseas are actually Cypriot, and this place near the Hilton Hotel shows why that island's food is popular, blending hearty Greek fare with Middle Eastern subtlety. Candlelight and music add a romantic touch.
✉ Zagoras 8 ☎ 778-5229
🕐 Daily dinner 🚌 230

Far East (££)
There are a number of Chinese restaurants in Athens and this is one of the best, with a vast menu which incorporates Japanese and Korean dishes alongside Chinese favourites such as hot and sour soup, sweet and sour pork, and crispy duck.
✉ Stadiou ☎ 323-4996
🕐 Daily lunch, dinner
🚇 Syntagma when opened

Five Brothers (£)
The Five Brothers restaurant has indoor and outdoor seating near the Roman Agora, various fixed-price options, generous portions and good grills and chops. A decent house wine and friendly waiters add to its appeal.
✉ Eolou 3 ☎ 325-0088 🕐 Daily 8AM–1AM 🚇 Monastiráki

GB Corner (£££)
Part of the Grande Bretagne Hotel (➤ 62, 101), this smart restaurant with piano bar serves a mix of good, traditional Greek cuisine and continental cooking. You get good food, good service and it's not over-priced.
✉ Grande Bretagne Hotel, Syntagma Square ☎ 331-4444 🕐 Daily 7AM–1AM 🚇 Syntagma when completed

Gerofinikas (££)
This smart and secluded place is one contender for the best food in Athens, with a strong Middle Eastern influence showing through in its use of lamb, chicken, yoghurt, spices, nuts, and rich desserts.
✉ Pindarou 10 ☎ 362-2719 🕐 Daily 12–11:30. Closed public holidays

Golden Flower (£)
An unpretentious Chinese restaurant, such as you find in every city in the world, this is reliable and inexpensive if you want noodles, crispy duck, sweet and sour dishes, prawn balls, shrimps and other Chinese staples.
✉ Nikis 30 ☎ 323-0113 🕐 Daily lunch, dinner 🚇 Syntagma when opened

Hermion (££)
This very pleasant and long-established café-restaurant is just off the flea market. It has indoor seating, an attractive courtyard dining area and excellent service of good-quality, moderately priced Greek favourites.
✉ Pandrossou 7–15 ☎ 324-6725 🕐 Daily breakfast, lunch, dinner 🚇 Monastiráki

Beyond the Pláka
You *can* eat well in the Pláka, and it does have one of the liveliest atmospheres in Athens, but if you really like your food you should explore the city's other areas. Some of the best restaurants – Greek and other cuisines – are in districts such as Theseion, Psirri, Metz and Kolonáki. Athens is one of the safest cities in the world, so explore; the only danger is to your waistline.

93

Greek Habits

Greeks eat late. Many places, especially in the Pláka, open early to cater for the tourist trade, but if you want to savour the real Athenian night atmosphere you won't consider arriving anywhere before about 9PM. Indeed, some of the more fashionable restaurants don't open until 8 or 9PM.

I Saita (£)

This unpretentious basement taverna offers wine from the barrel, murals, and a standard menu that occasionally features some delicious surprises, such as pork in a cream of celery sauce.

✉ Kydathinaion 21 🕓 Daily dinner 🚇 024, 230

Ideal (£££)

The Ideal is elegant and slightly expensive, but with attentive service and an extensive and interesting menu, including 'drunkard's titbits' (pork in tomato sauce with olives, onions, mushrooms and cheese) or prawns with feta.

✉ Panepestimiou 46 ☎ 330-2200 🕓 Mon–Sat 11–4:30, 8–2 🚇 Omonia

Kiku (££)

This rivals Michiko as the best Japanese restaurant in Athens, with sushi and sashimi prepared by Japanese chefs. Located in Kolonáki, it caters slightly more to business and diplomatic visitors than to tourists.

✉ Dimokritou 12 ☎ 364-7033 🕓 Daily lunch, dinner. Closed Sun lunch, midsummer 🚇 Syntagma when opened

Kona Kai (£££)

This restaurant in the Ledra Marriott Hotel specialises in Polynesian food (with décor as exotic as the dishes), but also has a Japanese menu. It's extremely popular, so booking is advisable.

✉ Syngrou 115 ☎ 934-7711 🕓 Mon–Sat dinner. Closed mid-August 🚇 2, 4, 11, 12

Kouklis (£)

Also known as To Yerani, this ouzerie is an established favourite, concentrating on hearty meze such as saganaki, taramasalata, fried fish and sausages cooked in ouzo. Also offers a pleasant dining terrace.

✉ Tripodon 14 ☎ 324-7605 🕓 Daily lunch, dinner 🚇 Monastiráki

L'Abreuvoir (£££)

This costly up-market French restaurant in Kolonáki, where Pavarotti and other celebrities have dined, has elegant decor and equally elegant food – steaks a speciality – and an extensive and expensive wine list.

✉ Xenokratous 51 ☎ 722-9061 🕓 Daily lunch, dinner 🚇 Syntagma when opened

Melrose (££)

No city is complete without its Pacific Rim restaurant, and this is Athens's finest. Seafood, naturally, is good – salmon, shrimps, swordfish – together with stylish décor and superb service.

✉ Zosimadou 16 (off Kallidromiou) ☎ 825-1627 🕓 Mon–Sat dinner. Closed August 🚇 Omonia

Michiko (££)

Set back from one of the Pláka's main streets, in a lovely mansion with a quiet courtyard, this tried and trusted favourite offers authentic Japanese cooking: sushi, sashimi, sukiyaki.

✉ Kydathinaion 27 ☎ 322-0980 🕓 Mon–Sat, lunch, dinner. Closed Sat lunch 🚇 024, 230

Mona Lisa (££)

Previously known as Jimmy's Cooking, this can be found in a romantic setting hidden away in Kolonáki. Ambitious pasta and fish dishes are a speciality, served with typical Italian hospitality.

✉ Loukianou 36 ☎ 724-7283 🕓 Daily lunch, dinner 🚇 Syntagma when opened

Myrtia (£££)

Although expensive for a taverna, the fixed-price menu here has countless courses so only come if you're incredibly hungry. There's music in the evening and the place will be packed. You can sit outside in summer.

✉ Trivonianou 32–34 ☎ 924-7181 🕐 Mon–Sat dinner. Closed August 🚇 2, 4, 11, 12

O Platanos (£)

This Athenian favourite offers few concessions to tourism, and has one of the best locations in the Pláka, with tables outside in the summer under the plane tree that provides its name.

✉ Diogenous 4 ☎ 322-0666 🕐 Mon–Sat 12–4:30, 8–12 🚇 Monastiráki

Orient (££)

Many Athenian restaurants serve a mix of Oriental food and this one is typical, with Korean, Chinese and Japanese dishes. It's not too expensive and is popular with locals as well as with tourists.

✉ Lekka 26 ☎ 322-1192 🕐 Daily lunch, dinner 🚇 Syntagma when opened

Palia Athina (££)

This is a simple, old-fashioned restaurant serving food, as one local described it, 'from mother's kitchen', with traditional items such as octopus in vinegar, grilled feta, pumpkin balls, fish soup, Florina peppers and squid.

✉ Nikis 46 ☎ 331-2975 🕐 Mon–Sat 12–1 🚇 024, 230

Palia Taverna (££)

Established in the late-19th century, and staying traditional in both its dishes and its atmosphere, there is often music, always good service, indoor and outdoor seating and a reliable menu.

✉ Markou Mousourou 36 ☎ 902-4493 🕐 Daily 7PM–2AM. Closed midsummer 🚇 2, 4, 11, 12

Piccolino ££

This is indistinguishable from the many other Pláka

restaurants that surround it, but has good service and good food: a generous appetiser of taramasalata, tzatziki, houmous, aubergine and potato salads.

✉ Sotiros 26/Kydathinaíon 10 ☎ 324-6692 🕐 Daily lunch, dinner 🚇 024, 230

Pil Poul (£££)

For the best of modern Greek cooking head for the Theseion and Psirri districts. This fashionable place, with dishes that reflect the whole Mediterranean, with Italian and Middle Eastern dashes, also offers Acropolis views.

✉ Apostolou Pavlou/Poulopoulou ☎ 342-3665 🕐 Mon–Sat dinner 🚇 Theseion

Prunier (££)

This French bistro near the Hilton Hotel offers a romantic setting in three rooms and typical bistro dishes, such as coq au vin and escargots. There are some more exotic choices too, like quail in oregano and lemon sauce.

✉ Ipsilantou 63 ☎ 722-7379 🕐 Mon–Sat dinner. Closed August 🚇 234

Senor Frog (££)

A lively and highly popular Mexican restaurant near the Gennadios Library, serving margaritas and Mexican beers, with chillies, fajitas and other hot specialities.

✉ Anapiron Polimou 10 ☎ 722-4524 🕐 Tue–Sun dinner 🚇 Syntagma when opened

Sigalas (£)

The bustle of the Pláka and flea markets seems to spill inside this century-old taverna. It's always busy, and is cheap, with a good range of Greek dishes, and frantic but good service.

✉ Plateía Monastiráki 2 ☎ 321-3036 🕐 Daily 7AM–2AM 🚇 Monastiráki

New Greek Cooking

If you think eating in Athens means only moussakas, think again. Try more upmarket restaurants for a wonderful surprise. I can still taste one meal at Ermou and Asomaton, which started with curried fried chicken, walnuts, mango, chicory and a cream, lemon, mustard and curry sauce, and was followed by a main course of pork filled with prunes and apricot, served with wild rice and a quince, apple and honey sauce. No moussakas on this menu!

A Tip
Greek menu prices are regulated by the Tourist Police and in many places you will find two prices listed: with and without tax. You pay the higher price. Smarter restaurants tend just to show the inclusive price. The tax is not a tip, and it is customary to leave the change, or some of it, when you pay the bill.

Socrates Prison (£)
Lively and justifiably popular for its unusual dishes, such as pork stuffed with vegetables, a fine house wine, home-made desserts, and outdoor seating.
✉ Mitseon 20 ☎ 922-3434 🕐 Daily 7PM–1AM. Closed August 🚌 230

Strofi (£)
With views of the Acropolis from the roof, this is understandably popular, serving good Greek staples.
✉ Rovertou Galli 25 ☎ 921-4130 🕐 Mon–Sat dinner 🚌 230

Symposio (£££)
Symposio combines superior food with a relaxed atmosphere and a very popular late-night bar in an elegant house. The menu blends international and Greek dishes, such as pasta with cheese from Metsovo.
✉ Erechthiou 46 ☎ 922-5321 🕐 Mon–Sat dinner 🚌 230

Ta Nissia (£££)
Superb views are matched by the food. Try the 'Mezedakia Experience' for a starter; it may also transport you for the evening! An expensive treat.
✉ Hilton Hotel, Vasilissis Sofias 46 ☎ 725-0201 🕐 7–12. Evenings only at time of writing – call before going for lunch 🚌 234

Taverna tou Psyrri (£)
One of the eating places that has transformed this district. The taverna's owner is from Naxos, which is reflected in his menu: good imported fish, meat and other produce.
✉ Aischylou 12 ☎ 321-4923 🕐 Daily lunch, dinner. Closed Sun dinner Ⓜ Monastiráki

To Cafenio (££)
This smart but relaxed restaurant serves excellent Greek specialities, such as spinach pie, baked aubergine with cheese, chicken in lemon sauce, to international diners, some from the nearby embassies.
✉ Loukianou 26 ☎ 723-7277 🕐 Mon–Sat lunch, dinner. Closed Aug 🚌 234

To Ypogeio tis Plakas (£)
A great basement place, with murals by local artist George Savakis. It has good, simple Greek food such as *souvlaki* and *calamaris*, and retsina straight from the barrel.
✉ Kydathinaion 10 ☎ 322-4304 🕐 Daily 7PM–2AM

Vitrina (£££)
This chic eatery in the newly fashionable Psirri area is setting the standards for both décor and food: lamb with mushrooms and red peppers in a sweet and sour port sauce is a regular dish.
✉ Navarchou Apostoli 7 ☎ 321-1200 🕐 Tue–Sat dinner, Sun lunch Ⓜ Monastiráki

White Elephant (££)
Based in the Andromeda Hotel, this is the place to come for something spicy; Szechuan and other Chinese dishes mix with Indian, Polynesian and Thai.
✉ Timoleontos Vassou 22 ☎ 643-7302 🕐 Mon–Sat dinner. Closed Jul–Aug 🚌 4

Xinos (££)
In a Pláka back street which few tourists find, this is very popular with Athenians, offering superior food, music and lovely outdoor garden.
✉ Angelou Geronta 4 ☎ 322-1065 🕐 Mon–Fri 8PM–12. Closed in winter

Zonar's (£)
Snacks, coffee, delicious pastries and light meals have been popular in this café since the 1930s.
✉ Panepistimiou 9 ☎ 323-0572 🕐 Daily 9AM–12:30AM

Outside Athens

Aígina (Aegina)

Kostas (£)

If in Ágia Marina to visit the nearby Temple of Aphaia, seek out this taverna with its attractive garden seating, not far from the beach. Friendly service and standard menu, but very well done.

✉ Ágia Marina ☎ 0297-32424 🕐 Daily lunch, dinner. **Closed winter**

Maridaki (£)

Lively waterfront restaurant-café where you can dine cheaply on salads or omelettes, moderately on grilled octopus or *moussaka*, or expensively on fresh fish, caught off Aígina that morning.

✉ Dimokratias ☎ 0297-25869 🕐 Daily, all day

Ákra Soúnio (Cape Sounion)

Ilias (££)

An alternative to the eating places outside the Temple of Poseidon is this fish taverna on the beach below. Less impressive view, but slightly cheaper. No surprises on the menu, but lots of good fresh fish.

✉ Ákra Soúnio ☎ 0292-39114 🕐 Daily lunch, dinner 🚌 Sounion bus

Delfoí (Delphi)

Iniochos (££)

This highly recommended establishment has superb views over the valley and a very good, varied menu in a town where poor tourist fare is the norm. The menu ranges from mussels and fresh fish to lamb in pastry and several vegetarian options.

✉ Frederikis 19 ☎ 0265-82710 🕐 Daily lunch, dinner

Taverna Arachova (£)

Home-grown food served in a small and very Greek place. Limited to mostly grills and salads, but they are well done and reasonably priced.

✉ Frederikis 50 ☎ 265-82452 🕐 Daily 6:30PM–12

Vakos (£)

Honest, unpretentious family-run taverna with friendly service and reliable versions of Greek favourites. No surprises, but good, with lovely views.

✉ Apollonos 31 ☎ 0265-82448 🕐 Daily lunch, dinner

Kifisiá (Kifissia)

Bokaris (££)

This renowned place in the smart northern suburb has a lovely outdoor seating area, a good wine list and good grilled meat and fish dishes.

✉ Sokratous 17 ☎ 801-2589 🕐 Daily 7PM–late, Sun lunch. **Closed August** 🚇 Kifisia

Vardis (£££)

In the Pentelikon Hotel is this elegant, costly, but good-quality French restaurant serving lobster, *filet mignon*, a range of other meat dishes and salads. A pianist plays in the evening.

✉ Deligianni 66 ☎ 808-0311 🕐 Daily lunch, dinner 🚇 Kifisia

Kórinthos (Corinth)

Pantheon (£)

A reliable local place in modern Corinth, where many cater to the passing tourist coach trade and standards can suffer. Offers good grills, staples such as *moussaka*, and generous salads.

✉ Ethnikis Antistasis ☎ 0741-25780 🕐 Daily lunch, dinner

Opening Times

Although we have given the opening details of all places at the time of writing, Greek restaurants and tavernas are capricious. Some close in winter, and some close in summer, or for a few weeks in midsummer. Some may decide to open, or close, for lunch. Others move premises. If planning a visit to one of these recommendations, please phone first to check it's open.

Seafood

Seafood is sold by weight, not a standard price per portion. If you simply ask for swordfish, you might be served a huge steak at a huge price. Tell the waiter how big a piece you want, or ask to see it before cooking, or go into the kitchen and choose for yourself. Have it weighed and priced, so that you do not receive a shock with the bill.

Mikínes (Mycenae)
La Belle Helene (££)
Eat here for a sense of place, as the restaurant is in the hotel Schliemann stayed at while excavating the site. There are no surprises on the menu, but the food is better than – if slightly pricier than – the many tourist-trap tavernas that abound.

☎ 0751-76225 ⏲ Daily lunch, dinner. Phone to check if open before going in the evening

Náfplio
Kakanarakis (£)
In a town where many tavernas are aimed purely at the tourist, this excellent place, two streets back from the waterfront, offers Greek specials even out of season: rabbit with feta, or squid in a wine sauce are just two examples.

✉ Vasilissis Olgas 18 ☎ 0752-25371 ⏲ Daily lunch, dinner

Karamanlis (£)
Here we have a seafront taverna that retains its Greekness, being away from the smarter end of the waterfront. The food is good, basic and inexpensive.

✉ Bouboulinas 1 ☎ 0752-27668 ⏲ Daily 11–12

Kipos (£)
Kipos means garden, and this friendly taverna has a lovely clean garden area off the narrow back street above Sindagma, shaded by a lemon tree and some vines. On offer is a conventional Greek menu of fish, grills and salads: well done and worth seeking out.

✉ Kapodistriou 8 ⏲ Daily lunch, dinner

Ta Phanaria (£)
A small shaded area by the side of this taverna provides a charming spot for a meal when visiting the town. Good vegetarian options alongside the Greek staples single out the Phanaria from some of the others in this taverna-lined street.

✉ Staikopoulou 13 ☎ 0752-27141 ⏲ Daily, all day

Savouras (££)
This waterfront place is one of the most popular fish restaurants in town, much praised by locals (who ought to know their fish). The menu varies with the season, naturally, but expect dishes such as mullet, bream and swordfish.

✉ Bouboulinas 79 ☎ 0752-27704 ⏲ Daily lunch, dinner

Zorba's (£)
This unpretentious taverna with friendly service and genuine home-cooking can be found in a street lined with tavernas that are hard to choose between. Zorba's offers moussaka as light as a feather and other simple dishes cooked by the wife and served by the easy-going husband.

✉ Staikopoulou 30 ☎ 0752-25319 ⏲ Daily lunch, evening

Peiraías (Piraeus)
Alli Skala (££)
Distinguished but, for Piraeus, not overpriced, this restaurant has a wonderful courtyard. On offer is a wider menu than just seafood, including meats and excellent examples of good Greek home cooking.

✉ Serifou 57 ☎ 482-7722 ⏲ Daily dinner 🚇 Piraeus

Dourambeis (£££)
One of the best in Piraeus, the Dourambeis was established in 1932. It's a simple restaurant but with outstanding – and expensive – fresh fish dishes from the Aegean islands, including a delicious crayfish soup.

✉ Athena Dilaveri 29 ☎ 412-2092 ⏲ Mon–Sat 8:30PM–1AM. Closed August 🚇 Piraeus

Kollias (££)
This renowned Piraeus fish restaurant offers friendly service and inspired cooking.
✉ Stratigou Plastira 3 ☎ 462-9620 🕐 Mon–Sat lunch, dinner. Closed August, lunch in summer 🚇 Piraeus

Mavri Gida (also called Kavos) (££)
Located in the Mikrolimano, this naturally specialises in fresh seafood, including lobster. It also has good game, such as venison and wild boar, in season.
✉ Akti Kounoundourou 64 ☎ 422-0691 🕐 Daily lunch, dinner 🚇 Piraeus

Panorama (££)
Near the Acropolis and away from the bustle of the harbour, here you can still get fresh fish (bream, mullet, swordfish) at reasonable prices with, as the name suggests, panoramic views.
✉ Irakliou 18–20 ☎ 417-3475 🕐 Daily lunch, dinner 🚇 Piraeus

Varoulko (£££)
Outstanding, elaborate, modern Greek/continental cuisine is served here, with an unusual menu featuring items such as vine leaves stuffed with fish, though monkfish is the chef's speciality. Booking is advised as there's often a queue. It's also very expensive.
✉ Deliyioryi 14 ☎ 411-2043 🕐 Mon–Sat 8PM–12. Closed August 🚇 Piraeus

Vasilenas (£)
Inexpensive places do exist in Piraeus if you forget fresh fish. This taverna has been here since the 1930s and is noted for its set menu of 16 different dishes that fill the stomach without emptying the wallet.
✉ Etolikou 72 ☎ 461-2457 🕐 Mon–Sat dinner 🚇 Piraeus

Póros
Caravella (£)
This very friendly (when not busy) waterfront taverna offers a typical, but well-prepared Greek menu.
✉ Paralia ☎ 0298-23666 🕐 Daily lunch, dinner

Spétses
Exedra (£)
Right on the harbour, this is one of the best of Spétses' many fine restaurants. While concentrating on fish, the Exedra cooks it with flair, and the menu includes a delicious shrimp, lobster and feta cheese bake, but also many vegetarian options.
✉ Old Harbour ☎ 0298-73497 🕐 Daily lunch, dinner

Lirakis (£)
Located above the Lirakis supermarket with a fine view of the harbour, the Lirakis has an eclectic menu ranging from omelettes and vegetarian dishes such as briam to more sophisticated, but traditionally Greek, meat and fish options.
✉ Main Harbour ☎ 0298-72188 🕐 Daily lunch, dinner. Closed winter

Ýdra (Hydra)
O Kipos (£)
This popular spot with a shady garden specialises in meat, including lamb in filo pastry, or goat. It also serves fresh fish and vegetarian dishes, reflecting the island's more cosmopolitan nature.
✉ Near stadium ☎ 0298-52329 🕐 Daily dinner. Closed winter

Xeri Elia (£)
Tucked down the narrow street near Kipos is this traditional taverna with a garden area, offering simple, but beautifully prepared dishes of meats and fresh fish, with friendly service.
✉ Off main square ☎ 0298-52886 🕐 Daily lunch, dinner

Hot or Warm?
Many places start cooking mid-morning, and some dishes, such as *moussaka* and stuffed tomatoes, may be cooked then and simply kept warm till lunch. This is not a cause for complaint, it is just the Greek way of doing things. If you want hot food guaranteed, choose something that needs to be freshly prepared, such as *souvlaki* or grilled fish.

Athens

Prices

Approximate prices per room per night:

£ = budget (under 10,000dr)

££ =moderate (10,000–20,000dr)

£££ =expensive (over 20,000dr)

Solo Travellers

Room rates in Athens are normally given per room, not per person. If you are travelling alone you may be asked to pay about three-quarters of the room rate for single occupancy, but this is at the discretion of the hotel and depends on availability and how busy they are.

It is common practice in Greece to ask to inspect a room before confirming a booking, so don't be afraid to ask. Smart receptions can mask down-at-heel rooms but, equally, a very ordinary lobby and reception area can lead to a perfectly pleasant establishment. Hotel frontages in Athens can be tiny, almost invisible, so don't always rely on first impressions.

Achilleas (££)

Newly refurbished and reasonably priced, this establishment is very close to Syntagma Square. All rooms are large and clean, *en suite*, with air-conditioning and telephones.

✉ **Lekka 21** ☎ **323-3197**
🚍 **Airport bus**

Acropolis House (££)

This inexpensive, family-run Pláka option is in a restored mansion. It is well maintained, though not all rooms have a bath.

✉ **Kodrou 6–8** ☎ **322-2344**
🚍 **Airport bus**

Acropolis View (£££)

This is a good, affordable up-market place on the south side of the Acropolis, which naturally means wonderful views of the site. All rooms are *en suite* with air-conditioning and telephones, and the hotel is in a quiet location.

✉ **Webster 10** ☎ **921-7303**
🚍 **Airport bus**

Adonis (££)

The Adonis is a good, standard, economic hotel with helpful staff, conveniently located in a pedestrian street right at the edge of the Pláka and not far from Syntagma Square. It has a breakfast room/bar with Acropolis views and attracts many regular visitors.

✉ **Kodrou 3** ☎ **324-9737**
🚍 **Airport bus**

Andromeda Athens (£££)

In a quiet street not far from the Temple of Olympian Zeus (► 55), this luxury hotel is aimed at the business traveller, with computers and fax machines available on request. It also features one of the best restaurants in town, the White Elephant (► 96).

✉ **Timoleondos Vassou 22** ☎ **643-7302** 🚍 **4**

Athenian Inn (££)

This long-established, quiet hotel is in the fashionable Kolonáki district, offering views of Lykabettos Hill from some rooms. It has traditional furnishings, is a favourite of authors and artists, but is not overpriced.

✉ **Haritos 22** ☎ **723-8097**
🚇 **Syntagma when completed**

Athens Hilton (£££)

Here you'll get typical Hilton high standards, and prices, but with an Athenian stamp – plants, restaurants and a meeting place for coffee. The hotel is convenient for Syntagma Square, the Benaki Museum (► 51) and the National Gallery (► 37), but not the Pláka.

✉ **Vasilissis Sofias 46** ☎ **725-0201** 🚇 **Syntagma when completed**

Attalos (££)

Simple, but clean and well-equipped, this Class C hotel offers friendly service and is very convenient for the Pláka, flea market and Monastiráki metro if you are heading for the ferries.

✉ **Athinas 29** ☎ 321-2801
🚇 **Monastiráki**

Carolina (£)

The Carolina is a budget establishment that has seen better days, but it is perfectly acceptable if funds are limited. Some rooms are *en suite* and most are small, but they are kept clean and the hotel makes a convenient central base for exploring the sights.

✉ **Kolokotroni 55** ☎ 324-0944 🚇 **Monastiráki**

Elektra Palace (£££)

The Elektra Palace is a real luxury option at the heart of the Pláka, with a rooftop pool and Acropolis views. All rooms have air-conditioning, TV, telephone and minibar. It's extremely comfortable and within walking distance of Syntagma Square and most of the main sights.

✉ **Nikodimou 18** ☎ 324-1401
🚌 **Airport bus**

Exarchion (£)

This inexpensive hotel is close to the National Archaeological Museum (► 18–19) in the lively student area of Exarchia. All rooms are *en suite* with air-conditioning, and many have a balcony.

✉ **Themistokleous 55** ☎ 380-1256 🚇 **Omonia**

Grande Bretagne (£££)

This is Athens's landmark hotel, where the guest register reads like a roll-call of history (► 62). Featuring marbled interiors, swimming pool, top restaurants, city views and impeccable service, it's also very expensive.

✉ **Plateía Syntagma** ☎ 323-0251 🚇 **Syntagma when completed**

Herodion (£££)

Despite being on the south side of the Acropolis away from the Pláka, this smart hotel has several highly recommended restaurants near by. All rooms are *en suite* with TV and telephone, and the hotel's rooftop terrace has lovely views of the Parthenon.

✉ **Rovertou Gali 4** ☎ 923-6832 🚌 **230**

Imperial (££)

Despite the name and location, close to Syntagma Square and overlooking Mitrópolis, this is a moderately priced hotel with a friendly staff and clean rooms. It's also within walking distance of most of the main sights.

✉ **Mitropoleos 40** ☎ 322-7617 🚇 **Monastiráki**

King Minos (££)

This large, refurbished hotel has clean rooms, all with air-conditioning and telephones. Facilities also include a bar, restaurant and lounges.

✉ **Pireos 1** ☎ 523-1111
🚇 **Omonia**

Kouros (£)

The Kouros is ideally placed in a street with several small hotels: quiet but just a few metres from the heart of the Pláka. It offers no frills, but the rooms are clean. The hotel was formerly a mansion and there is lots of tourist literature available.

✉ **Kodrou 11** ☎ 322-7431
🚌 **Airport bus**

Marble House Pension (££)

Just a short walk from the southern side of the Acropolis is this quiet, friendly and inexpensive little hotel. Half the rooms are *en suite*, some have vine-covered balconies, all are clean, and the owners are extremely helpful.

✉ **Zinni 35a** ☎ 923-4058 🚌 **Airport bus**

Meet the Author!

You might bump into the author of this book if you stay at the Attalos Hotel, just up from Monastiráki Square. It's my favourite place to stay in Athens, combining inexpensive, clean rooms with friendliness and convenience. Any comments about the guidebook – or the hotel – will be gratefully received. Preferably in the rooftop bar.

Not-So-Grande Bretagne

When the Grande Bretagne Hotel was built in the late 19th century, it was called the 'Petit Palais' as the Greek royal family used it to house their guests when the Royal Palace was full. It did have one disadvantage, however – there was only one bathroom, in the basement. Today it is acknowledged as one of Europe's great hotels.

La Mirage (££)

On Omonia Square but shielded from the noise, all rooms here are *en suite* with telephone, air-conditioning and minibars. The Mirage is a good, well-maintained hotel, with a restaurant, bar and lounges. It offers reasonable rates for those who want to be in amongst the bustle.

✉ Kotopouli 3 ☎ 523-4755
🚇 Omonia

Museum (£)

Behind the National Archaeological Museum, but overlooking its gardens, this quiet and well-maintained hotel is a good affordable option if you want to be in this area. All rooms are *en suite* and have a telephone.

✉ Bouboulinas 16 ☎ 380-5611 🚇 Omonia

Nefeli (££)

This is a small, family-run hotel of just 18 rooms. With many regular visitors, it is inexpensive, friendly, modern, spotlessly clean and convenient for both the Pláka and the city centre.

✉ Yperidou 16 ☎ 322-8044
🚌 Airport bus

Omonia (£)

Busy and big, this budget but acceptable choice on Omonia Square may be a little worn at the edges, but it is kept spotlessly clean. All rooms have showers and phones, and some have balconies.

✉ Omonia ☎ 523-7211
🚇 Omonia

Orion (£)

The Orion is very cheap, but is a perfectly acceptable place if you're travelling on a strict budget. Located in the lively Exarchia district (▶ 38), it is great for student nightlife but a long walk from the Omonia metro.

✉ Emmanuel Benaki 105
☎ 382-7362 🚇 Omonia

Philippos (££)

This is a good mid-range choice for the Makriyanni district, south of the Acropolis and close to several excellent restaurants. All rooms are *en suite*, with phones, TVs and air-conditioning.

✉ Mitseon 3 ☎ 922-3611
🚌 Airport bus

Pláka (£££)

A slightly pricier Pláka hotel, but very smart, clean, modern and bright. Extremely well located close to Mitropoleos, some rooms have views of the Acropolis, as does the roof garden.

✉ Kapnikareas 7 ☎ 322-2096 🚇 Monastiráki

Royal Olympic (£££)

At the cheaper end of its price range, this large hotel, close to many major sights, has large air-conditioned rooms with TV and phone.

✉ Odos Diakou 28 ☎ 922-6411 🚇 Syntagma when opened

Tempi (££)

Very central, this small, clean budget place is popular with students and others who prefer a friendly atmosphere to frills, though some rooms have showers. It is handy for Monastiráki Square.

✉ Eolou 29 ☎ 321-3175
🚇 Monastiráki

Titania (£££)

This huge hotel with high standards is handily placed for both Omonia and Syntagma Squares, a short walk from the Pláka and the National Archaeological Museum (▶ 18–19). It offers well-equipped rooms, room service, a restaurant and a roof bar with views of the Acropolis. A bonus for drivers is parking space for 400 cars.

✉ Panepistimiou 52 ☎ 330-0111 🚇 Omonia

Outside Athens

Aígina (Aegina)
Aeginitiko Archontiko (£)
Located in a restored traditional mansion, which was first built in 1820, this hotel is stronger on atmosphere than on the quality of its rooms. But it represents a perfectly acceptable and economic option and is conveniently placed in the centre of Aegina Town.

✉ Eakou 1 ☎ 0297-24968

Ákra Soúnio (Cape Sounion)
Aegaeon (££)
The Aegaeon is very well placed for enjoying Sounion's bay and, above, the famous temple. It's a clean and spacious hotel right on the beach, and features a good restaurant and moderate prices.

✉ Ákra Soúnio ☎ 0292-39262 🚌 Sounion bus

Delfoí (Delphi)
Olympic (££)
The Olympic is a lovely old-fashioned establishment with immaculate furnishings and stunning views. It has 25 en suite rooms. It enjoys a central location, close to some of Delphi's better restaurants.

✉ Frederikis 57/Kingpol 53 ☎ 0265-82163

Varonos (£)
The Varonos is a very small, family-run hotel and makes an ideal choice for the independent traveller on a budget. Visitors are well looked after by extremely friendly owners, and it offers basic but clean rooms and superb views.

✉ Pavlou and Frederikis 27 ☎ 0265-82345

Kórinthos (Corinth)
Bellevue (£)
The front rooms at the Bellevue may have harbour views, but they also have noise. However, the owners run a good hotel for its class. Few rooms are *en suite*, but prices reflect this in a place where rates can be overly high.

✉ Damaskinou 41 ☎ 0741-22068

Marathónas (Marathon)
Golden Coast (£££)
Well located close to the Marathon sites, and on the beach, the Golden Coast represents a first-class option for anyone wanting to be near, but not in, Athens. The hotel features four pools, a nightclub and watersports facilities.

✉ Marathónas Beach ☎ 0294-57100 🚌 Marathon bus

Hotel Marathon (£)
Close to the Marathon sites and the beach, this is a good, clean and rather old-fashioned establishment, especially for visitors taking a short break from the bustle of Athens.

✉ Timvos Beach ☎ 0294-55122 🚌 Marathon bus

Mikínes (Mycenae)
La Belle Helene (££)
This is the long-established hotel in which the archaeologist Heinrich Schliemann stayed while excavating Mycenae, up the road. It is simple but clean, with eight rooms, none of them *en suite*, but its terrific character makes up for the basic amenities.

✉ Mykines ☎ 0751 62257

Room Rate
Each bedroom in a Greek hotel must display a notice giving the room rate for the various periods of the year, which is approved by the Tourist Police. If you're paying less, it may be because business is slow, but if you're paying more than the notice says, you might want to query it. One possible explanation is breakfast: sometimes this is an optional extra, sometime a compulsory extra, and sometimes included in the price.

Haggling

Haggling is part of Athenian life in the tourist areas, though not quite as much as in, say, the Middle East. In the Pláka you would be crazy (and the Greeks would think you so) to pay the first price you're quoted for anything, even the 'Special price today for you my friend'. Offer half, and be prepared to meet in the middle. Don't feel guilty – remember, the shopkeeper will never lose out on a deal.

Náfplio

Byron (££)

Named after the poet is this brightly painted, intimate hotel in a back street, opposite the entrance to Ágios Spyridon church. It has 13 rooms, all with bath and phone, and lots of personality.

✉ **Plateía Ágiou Spiridona** ☎ **0752-22351**

King Otto (£)

This old favourite has 12 simple, inexpensive rooms, some overlooking the courtyard garden where breakfast is served. The minimal amenities are compensated for by the old-world atmosphere. Closed in winter.

✉ **Farmakopoulon 3** ☎ **0752-27585**

Peiraiás (Piraeus)

Ideal (££)

Hotels in Piraeus can be expensive or seedy, but the Ideal is neither, and it's also handy for the international ferry ports. It has 29 *en suite* rooms, which are clean and have phones and air conditioning. It's worth booking ahead if you need to spend a night in Piraeus.

✉ **Notara 142** ☎ **451-1727**
🚌 **Airport bus**

Lilia (££)

The Lilia is slightly pricier than the Ideal (► above), but has a more pleasant setting away from the noisy waterfronts. Its rooms are just as clean and comfortable. The closest harbour is Zea Marina, used by hydrofoils and catamarans to many destinations.

✉ **Zeas 131** ☎ **417-9108**
🚌 **Airport bus**

Póros

Latsi (£)

It may be budget and basic, but the Latsi is a comfortable place in which to stay on an island where the tourist trade bumps up prices. Most of the 39 rooms are *en suite* and some have lovely views across the straits to the Peloponnese.

✉ **Papadopoulou 74** ☎ **0298-22392**

Rafína

Hotel Avra (£££)

This is the best hotel in town, with welcoming staff, and makes a very pleasant place for a break while in Rafina. Some rooms have sea views and all are *en suite*, with air-conditioning and telephones.

✉ **Rafina** ☎ **0294-22781**

Spétses

Poseidon (£££)

The great Greek god of the sea Poseidon himself would enjoy this charming hotel, overlooking the harbour and offering views across to the mainland. Delightfully old-fashioned, but with a slightly fading grandeur, it has great charm and character.

✉ **Dapia waterfront** ☎ **0298-72006** 🕓 **Winter**

Ýdra (Hydra)

Bratsera (£££)

If you've ever felt the urge to stay in a former sponge factory, then be sure not to miss this opportunity. The Bratsera is an excellent conversion, featuring traditional island décor, swimming pool, and garden dining area; and it's close to the main harbour.

✉ **Tombazi** ☎ **0298-53971**

Antiques, Arts & Crafts

Aidini
This is a small but distinctive craft workshop and gallery, where the owner makes and sells his own metalwork, including strange fish, hanging aeroplanes and rather surreal sculptures.
✉ Nikis 32 ☎ 323-4591/ 322-6088

To Anoyi
The owner of this studio specialises in her own painted icons and eggs, but also sells the work of other Greek artists: ceramics, sculptures, blankets and wall-hangings.
✉ Sotiros 1 ☎ 322-6487

L'Atelier
Here you'll find good copies of Greek antiquities, such as vases, frescoes and Cycladic statues. You may be lucky enough to see these instant 'antiques' being made.
✉ Adrianou 116 ☎ 323-3740

The Athens Gallery
In among the Pláka shops all selling identical items is this stylish gallery representing the work of a handful of contemporary Greek artists. The gallery is expensive but exquisite.
✉ Pandrossou 14 ☎ 324-6942/894-0217

Centre of Hellenic Tradition
Between Metropoleos and Pandrossou, this arcade houses a selection of small shops devoted to Greek arts and crafts, including paintings, ceramics, wood-work and icons. It also has an enjoyable and often quiet café.
✉ Metropóleos 59/Pandrossou 36 ☎ 321-3023/3842

EOMMEX
This is a co-operative that specialises in handmade rugs produced on traditional looms by weavers from all over Greece.
✉ Metropóleos 9 ☎ 323-0408

Gallerie Areta
A small offshoot of the Athens Gallery (▶ above), the Areta contains mainly ceramics and paintings, including some delightful primitive artwork.
✉ Pandrossou 31 ☎ 324-3397/894-0217

Goutis
An unusual range of crafts and gifts, such as distinctive shadow puppets, traditional jewellery, blankets and pottery can be found here.
✉ Pandrossou 40 ☎ 321-3212

Greek Women's Institution
This outlet helps to keep alive the Greek embroidery tradition, providing remote rural and island communities with some benefit from tourism, which they may not otherwise receive.
✉ Ypatias 6 ☎ 325-0524

Iakovos Antiques
On offer are ceramics, paintings and knick-knacks, not just from Greece but from around the world.
✉ Ifestou 6 ☎ 321-0169

Karamikos Mazarakis
As well as traditional Greek *flokati* rugs and *kilims*, this large shop sells wool and silk rugs from the rest of the world, including unusual contemporary rugs based on designs by Dali, Picasso, Magritte and other artists.
✉ Voulis 31–33 ☎ 322-4932

Bric-à-Brac
Good junk shops selling artworks, old prints and postcards are to be found at the very far end of Adrianou, beyond the Tower of the Winds, away from the souvenir shops of the Pláka.

Museum Copies
Several of the major museums in Athens sell copies of their most appealing items, and these can range from small and inexpensive to life-size reproductions. Standards are generally very high indeed and the main shops which should be visited are at the National Archaeological Museum (▶ 18–19), the Benaki Museum (▶ 51) and the Goulandris Museum of Cycladic Art (▶ 24).

Exporting

It is illegal to export antiques from Greece, but there is an illicit trade in antiquities and ancient icons, which are much desired by collectors. If offered an alleged antique, you should consider whether it is genuine anyway, what will happen at customs, and the morality of smuggling antiquities that may be stolen or excavated illegally. A prison sentence can be imposed for this offence. Lord Elgin would never get through customs these days!

Kostas Sokaras
This sells an intriguing mix of embroidery, jewellery, Greek folk costumes and traditional shadow theatre puppets.
✉ Adrianou 25 ☎ 321-6826

Motakis
This sprawling junk/antique shop in a sizeable basement is typical of the Pláka. Established for almost a century, it sells everything from exquisite antiques to offbeat curios.
✉ Platia Abyssinia 3 ☎ 321-9005

Museum of Greek Children's Art
You can get unusual and charming gifts for the art lover at this museum, where prize-winning paintings by Greek children are both on display and for sale. Can you spot the talents of the future?
✉ Kodrou 9 ☎ 331-2621

Nasiotis
Look for the display of old photos, engravings, books, magazines and saucy postcards in this Aladdin's cave. Beneath is a cavernous jumble of books.
✉ Ifestou 24 ☎ 321-2369

National Welfare Organisation
This excellent scheme offers for sale traditional craftwork (embroidery, rugs, ceramics and icons) and also practical items, such as kitchenware, made by rural communities throughout Greece.
✉ Ypatias 6 ☎ 325-0524

Olive Wood Workshop
This crafts outlet is a delightful little family shop in a Pláka side street selling beautiful olive-wood carvings, including bread boards, cheese boards and bowls, most of which are made by the owner.
✉ Mnisikleous 8 ☎ 321-6145

Panayiri
If visiting Kolonáki, look for this shop, with its range of craft and gift items, paintings and books. It specialises in ships carved by the owner in wood salvaged from old ships.
✉ Kleomenous 25 ☎ 722-5369

Pyromania
Unlikely name for a fine art and crafts shop, but there are some tasteful examples of handblown glass, ceramics and olive-wood carvings, with a small workshop at the rear where the artist-owner may be at work.
✉ Kodrou 14 ☎ 325-5288

Riza
Not cheap, but sells fine examples of hand-made lace, as well as more affordable machine-produced work, glassware and other items from contemporary Greek craftspeople.
✉ Voukourestiou 35 ☎ 361-1157

Spiro Aravantinos
Superbly hand-crafted children's toys, dolls and puppets.
✉ Nikodimou 9 ☎ 323-6363

Takis Moraytis
Shop of Pláka artist, displaying some attractive Greek scenes. Originality like this is a little expensive compared to the prices of the mass-produced pictures in surrounding shops, but you get what you pay for!
✉ Adrianou 129 ☎ 322-5208

Vassilios Kervorkian
Even if you have no intention of buying one of the hand-made musical instruments on display in this small shop, you should stop to admire the skill that goes into the production of these guitars, bouzoukis and other items.
✉ Ifestou 6 ☎ 321-0024

Reading & Music

Books, Newspapers & Magazines

The Booknest
Reflected in its rather quaint name, this is a lovely jumble of a bookshop that stocks hardbacks and paperbacks, old and new, guidebooks and fiction, in many languages.
✉ **Panepistimiou 25–29** ☎ **323-1703**

Compendium
Here you'll find English-language books, magazines, guides, fiction, books about Greece, maps and a large second-hand section for exchanging your used paperbacks. There's a notice-board for language courses, apartments to rent etc. The shop also features occasional evening readings by local and visiting writers.
✉ **Nikis 25** ☎ **322-1248**

Lexis
On offer here is a decent selection of foreign-language paperbacks, in a street that is good for bookshops, though mostly of Greek-language books.
✉ **Akadimias 82** ☎ **384-5823/0844**

Pantelides
This is probably the biggest English-language bookshop in Athens, with a knowledgeable owner and stock ranging from popular blockbusting paperbacks to obscure specialist works. There's a good section covering books about Greece, plus dictionaries, art books, cookery and history books.
✉ **Amerikis 11** ☎ **362-3673**

Raymondos
Raymondos offers a very wide range of foreign magazines, some books in foreign languages and is a good source of magazines about Greece, such as *Odyssey* and *Atlantis*, Greek fiction in English and guidebooks.
✉ **Voukourestiou 18** ☎ **364-8189**

Music

Music is part of the Greek soul, although the tourist shops in the Pláka tend to stock only a limited range of compilations of Greek 'classics', like *Zorba the Greek* and *Never on Sunday*. Greek music is more varied than that, and a good way to get a feel for it is to visit the Museum of Greek Musical Instruments (➤ 23) and then go into the museum shop to examine the enormous range of CDs, LPs and books on sale.

In the Monastiráki flea market there are several specialist record shops, with a particular emphasis on 1960s and 1970s music, from the popular to the obscure. You will find a good selection of vinyl as well as CDs.

Museum of Greek Musical Instruments
The museum shop does not sell instruments but recordings, covering every type of musical tradition from all over Greece. There is also a good stock of books on music and Greek dancing, though mainly in Greek. (➤ 23).
✉ **Diogenous 1–3** ☎ **325-0198**

Just Browsing
Although it doesn't happen as frequently in Athens as it does in Middle Eastern countries, don't be surprised if the shop owner offers you a cup of tea or coffee. This is an old tradition in this part of the world, and is a mix of courtesy and common sense: while you enjoy your drink, the owner has more chance of selling you something.

Clothing & Jewellery

Clothing

The newly pedestrianised Ermou area has a range of Greek and international clothes shops, such as Benetton, Lacoste, Next and Marks & Spencer. More exclusive designer shops can be found in the more up-market Kolonáki district, at the foot of Lykabettos Hill.

Artisti Italiani
No surprises here: stylish Italian designs for women and men, priced accordingly.
✉ **Kanari 5** ☎ **363-9085**

DKNY
If you don't know what the initials stand for, you probably can't afford to shop there.
✉ **Dimokritou 34** ☎ **363-6188**

Jade
Fashionable shop exclusively for women.
✉ **Anagnostopoulou 3** ☎ **364-5922**

Laura Ashley
The famous British chain selling women's clothes that are stylish but safe.
✉ **Herodotou 28** ☎ **724-6869**

Stavros Melissinos
Now a Pláka institution, Melissinos has been creating both sandals and poetry since the 1960s. He has made sandals for John Lennon and sent his poetry to the White House. The master cobbler will hand-make a pair of sandals for you if there is nothing in his cramped and well-stocked quarters that fits the bill, or your feet.
✉ **Pandrossou 89** ☎ **321-9247**

Jewellery

Athens has a long tradition of silversmiths, and a number of shops can be found in the district around Lekka and Praxitelous streets. Some of these have such huge garish silver displays that it might be advisable to wear sunglasses. However, there are some smaller shops which include rather more tasteful items. Several of the more expensive jewellery shops are along the pleasant pedestrianised Voukouretiou shopping street.

Borell's
Modern and some antique jewellery on offer, just off Kolonáki Square and with Kolonáki prices.
✉ **Ypsilandou 5** ☎ **721-9772**

Ilias Lalaounis Jewellery Museum
Buy copies of works by this world-famous Greek jewellery designer in this stylish new museum devoted to his collections. Originals can be ordered, at a price. The Museum Shop is at Panepistimiou 6, ☎ 361-1371.
✉ **Karyatidon-Kallisperi 12** ☎ **922-1044**

Nisiotis
Excellent shop specialising in up-market silverware.
✉ **Lekka 23** ☎ **324-4183**

Zolotas
One of Greece's leading jewellers, and even if you cannot afford the items, the jewellery on sale is worth seeing in its own right. Also now has a shop in the Pláka at Pandrossou 8.
✉ **Stadiou 9** ☎ **322-1222**

Food & Drink

What to Buy

The best food buys in Greece are olive oil and honey, though the latter is not especially cheap. It is especially good, however. Spirits are often sold at very low prices in the country. Ceramics and leather are also good buys, as are handicrafts such as lace and *flokati* – the hand-woven woollen rugs. There is also a big trade in museum copies and in modern icons. Distinctive Greek items include worry beads (*kombolói*) and the long-handed copper pots used for making Greek coffee.

Visit the Central Market (▶ 40) for a great selection of herbs, spices, nuts, olives, cheeses and similar delicacies. It's a good place to visit to stock up with everything for a cheap picnic lunch. You could do the same at the Prisunic Marinopoulos supermarket chain, which offers a good range of produce. The stores are distinguished by the large orange 'M' sign.

Greece has a long tradition of the village shop that sells everything, so if you're directed to the 'supermarket' do not necessarily expect to find the huge American-style shopping experience. An experience it may be, as the shopkeeper delves into the dusty stock to search for what you want – and often succeeding – but not on the American scale of things. Supermarkets here are also mini-markets, especially in the tourist areas, again selling everything you might possibly need – and probably a great deal you won't.

Aristokratikon
You can indulge yourself here with a luxury range of chocolates, nougat, nuts and Turkish delight.
✉ **Karayioryi Servias 9**
☎ **322-0546**

Asimakopouli
This renowned Athenian patisserie is a must for anyone with an extremely sweet tooth. Greeks like their sweets sweeter than most.
✉ **Charilaou Trikoupi 82**
☎ **361-0092**

Bachar
Bachar is a specialist shop, near the Central Market, concentrating on a large range of spices and herbs for both culinary and medicinal use.
✉ **Evripidou 31** ☎ **321-7225**

Brettos
This well-stocked drinks shop in the Pláka district specialises in own-brand spirits and liqueurs as well as a wide range of Greek drinks such as ouzo and Metaxa.
✉ **Kydathinaion 41** ☎ **323-2110**

Katsarou
This store is slightly out of the centre, near the Larissis railway station, but is worth seeking out if you want to stock up on reasonably priced Greek drinks, anything from aperitifs through wines to brandies.
✉ **Liossion 89** ☎ **821-1767**

Koroni
This superior drinks shop in Náfplio stocks international brands and a range of up-market Greek wines.
✉ **Amalias 6 , Náfplio**

Greek Wine
The wines of Greece have never gained an international reputation, as most Greeks are happy with the resinated flavour of *retsina*, and many prefer beer or soft drinks. However, in recent years the standard has improved considerably thanks to tourism and increased demand by more discerning and affluent Greeks.

Children's Athens

Love Affair

Greeks love children. They are indulgent towards them and if a child is behaving a little badly, they accept that this is the way children sometimes are. They seldom scold children, and if you are seen to scold your child, they will make no comment but will inwardly disapprove. Don't be embarrassed if your child is behaving badly, as it is more likely to be greeted with a smile than a frown of disapproval.

Part of the Family

As in most Mediterranean countries, children are part of the family and will go with their parents – and grandparents and cousins – to eat in the evening. Don't be afraid to take your child into a restaurant, no matter how smart. And don't be surprised to see Greek children out late at night. Do the same with your child, but adopt the Greek habit and have an afternoon rest.

Aquarium

Not worth the journey from central Athens, but certainly worth knowing about if there are unexpected flight delays or long waits at the airport. There are several tanks of exotic fish and a crocodile named Kosmos. A short taxi ride from outside the airport.

✉ Ágios Kosmos Sports Area ☎ 894-5640 ⏰ Mon–Fri 10–3 🚌 Airport bus

Beaches

While adults are attracted to Athens for its cultural sites, your visit can be turned into a family holiday by choosing a hotel in one of the coastal suburbs. Places like Glyfada provide sea and sand, and it's easy to get to and from the city centre using buses or fairly cheap taxis. Alternatively, base yourself in the centre and take a taxi out for a day at the seaside. A cheaper option is to catch the airport bus, and then pick up a taxi from the airport. At Astir Beach there are plenty of watersports to amuse all the family, plus good shopping and numerous places to eat. The suburbs of Varkiza, Voula and Vouliagmeni also have good beach facilities.

Goulandris Natural History Museum

A journey to Kifissia should keep children happy for at least half a day, as it not only combines a ride on the metro but can include a visit to this excellent museum. There are good displays on environmental problems, some of which are caused by tourism – a lesson that travellers are never too young to learn. There are

also extensive collections on Greek flora and fauna, including some of the larger birds of prey and mammals such as bears and wolves, which few visitors will ever see in the wild.

✉ Levidou 13 ☎ 808-6405 ⏰ Sat, Sun 9–2. Currently closed weekdays, public holidays 🚇 Kifisia

Hellenic Children's Museum (➤ 36)

Contact the Museum for details of current activities. Although some of the staff speak English and welcome children of all ages and nationalities, advance notice for visits by non-Greek speaking children is advisable.

✉ Kydathinaion 14 ☎ 331-2995 ⏰ Fri–Mon and Wed 10–5. Closed public holidays 🚇 Syntagma when opened

Lykabettos Hill (➤ 21)

Though children are not normally gripped for long by panoramic views over cities, such as you get from the top of Lykabettos Hill, they will probably enjoy the journey up there if you take them on the funicular. The only drawback may be that they will want to come straight back down again, without allowing you time to enjoy the view. Persuade them to stay with a drink in one of the cafés at the top.

✉ Plutarhou ⏰ Daily 8–10

Museum of Greek Children's Art (➤ 52)

This small, lively museum has displays of art that includes imaginative sculptures, as well as tables and materials for children to use.

✉ Kodrou 9 ☎ 331-2621 ⏰
Tue–Sat 10–2, Sun 11–2. Closed
public holidays 🚇 Syntagma
when opened

Museum of Greek Musical Instruments (➤ 23)

While it isn't possible to
actually play any of the
instruments in this valuable
collection, you can listen to
most of them on
headphones provided at
each case. Videos are also
shown, illustrating how
various instruments are
made and played.

✉ Diogenous 1–3 ☎ 325-
0198/4119 ⏰ Tue, Thu–Sun
10–2, Wed 12–6. Closed public
holidays 🚇 Monastiráki

National Gardens (➤ 37)

In addition to simply
exploring the gardens,
perhaps looking for small
ponds where fish and
terrapins live, there is also a
Children's Library in the
centre of the gardens:
signposted from the main
entrance on Amalias. Adults
are not admitted, and there
are books, toys, tapes and
games in Greek, English and
other languages.

⏰ Closed Mon, public
holidays

Olympic Stadium (➤ 26)

The running track of the
1896 Olympic Stadium is
open to anyone to use during
the day, and children might
enjoy races around the track
or even up the steep seating
and down again.

✉ Leoforus Ardhittou ⏰
Daily sunrise–sunset 🚌 4,
11, 12

Piraeus and the Islands

A good day out – and a good
way of tiring children out – is
to make a day trip to one or
more of the Argo-Saronic
islands. An early start will
mean a ride on the metro to
Piraeus (➤ 86), and then the
excitement of a journey on
one of the hydrofoils to
Aegina, Póros, Spétses
or Hydra.

🚇 Piraeus

Shopping

There are plenty of shops in
Athens which will appeal to
children, perhaps allowing
parents to alternate with
some shopping of their own.
See the Shopping section
(➤ 105–9) for details of the
following: Spiro Aravantinos
(children's toys), Goutis and
Kostas Sokaras (puppets),
Panayiri (model boats)
and bookshops like
Compendium, which has a
good range of children's
books in a special room and
also organises readings on
two Saturdays each month.
These would mostly be in
Greek, but readings in other
languages also take place.

Syntagma Square

The Changing of the Guard is
a dramatic precision routine
that fascinates young and old
alike. It takes place hourly
(11AM only on Sundays) in
front of the Parliament
Building at the top of the
square. While waiting,
younger children will
probably enjoy chasing or
feeding the pigeons.

Theatre

As well as the Greek Theatre
Museum (➤ 42), which has
enjoyable displays of stage
sets and dressing rooms,
there are also various theatre
groups in Athens. The
English-language daily, *The
Hellenic Times*, has a 'Kids
Corner' section which lists
these and other ideas for
entertaining children. The
English Theatre Club ☎
363-1217/724-8219, for
example, is aimed at Greek
children wanting to improve
their English by putting on
performances. Children
would be very welcome to
attend and join in the fun.

Amusement Parks and Playgrounds

Mobile amusement parks
may pop up anywhere in
Athens at any time, so
keep a look out, ask
around, or buy one of the
city's listings magazines
for current information.
Summer usually sees
outdoor cinemas
appearing in parks and on
waste land too. Take a trip
out to the beach suburb of
Glyfada for more
permanent playgrounds.
There is also one in the
National Gardens, and in
the grounds of Lykabettos
Hill, near the Gennadios
Library (➤ 38).

Entertainment & Nightlife

Food, Drink, Prices
Many clubs have an admission fee which may sometimes include the cost of your first drink, while others have a minimum cover charge to prevent people occupying a table just for the music. Some serve food and some don't. Some take table reservations and some don't. In most cases, prices are pretty high, and any food served is usually fairly average.

General

Athens has several English-language listings magazines, such as *Athens Today* and *Scope Weekly*, providing up-to-date information on what's happening in the city. There are also weekly and daily English-language newspapers, and a German-language weekly. There are Greek-language publications too, available at most newsagents and kiosks. If in difficulty, try around Syntagma Square.

The more cultural glossy magazines, for example, *Atlantis* and *Odyssey*, also have news of movies, galleries, music and other entertainment options.

Casinos

On top of Mount Parnes, an hour's drive north of Athens, is one of Europe's biggest casinos. Evening dress and a valid passport are required for admission to the casino. Closed Wed.
☎ 246-9111

Festivals

Each summer sees the Athens Festival, which includes all the major art forms, and incorporates some music and theatrical performances, held in the theatre at Epídavros (▶ 80) as well as the Herodes Atticus Theatre below the Acropolis. Modern plays are staged in addition to classical Greek drama (seen in the settings for which it was written). Get a current programme and book tickets at the box office (Mon–Fri), which opens especially for the Festival. If you want to take a chance, any unsold tickets are usually available at the Herodes Atticus Theatre box office from about 6PM on the evening of the performance.

Overlapping the start of the Athens Festival is the Athens International Jazz and Blues Festival, tickets for which are available at the same box office on Stadiou.
✉ Stadiou 4 ☎ 322-1459

Movies

Athens has a few dozen cinemas in and around the centre, and you can see new movies here as quickly as anywhere in Europe. They are usually performed in the original language with Greek subtitles added, but check first as some may be dubbed into Greek.

In summer the conventional cinemas are augmented by temporary outdoor cinemas, set up on waste ground, in car parks and on rooftops. You will see signs for these as you walk around, and will certainly hear them if you pass by during an early performance; late-night shows have to turn down the volume level.

Sound and Light

A superb sight at any time, the Acropolis is illuminated and on show from the theatre on Filopáppou Hill, clearly marked from the entrance opposite the southern slopes of the Acropolis.
☎ 322-4128 🕐 1 Apr–31 Oct. **English nightly 9; German, Tue, Thu 10; French 10 all other nights.**

There are countless music venues in Athens, from classical concert halls to *rembetika* clubs, tucked away all over the city. There are also jazz clubs, blues clubs, rock venues, discos, dance clubs and innumerable places putting on traditional Greek music, whether for those who prefer the safety of a popular tourist venue, or those who want the real thing in the company of Athenians. Buy one of the many listings magazines such as *Scope Weekly* for further details, or look for posters in record shops such as Metropolis (Panepistimiou 64), Virgin (Stadiou 7–9) and the many small stores in the Monastiráki flea market.

Classical Music

The Greek National Opera
Their established home is at the Olympia Theatre along Akadimias, but the company also puts on ballet performances here.
✉ **Akadimias 59** ☎ **361-2461**

Mégaron Athens Concert Hall
This bright new building was opened in 1991 and presents ballet, opera and classical music, including performances by the Athens State Orchestra and visiting companies.
✉ **Vas. Sofias and Kokkali** ☎ **728-2333**

Jazz

Half Note
Live jazz is on offer most nights from international bands in this well-established venue in the Mets district (west of the Stadion). The club opens at 10, but beware the hefty admission fee.
✉ **Trivonianou 17** ☎ **923-2460/921-3310** 🕓 **Closed Tue, summer**

Jazz Club Diva
This smart and relaxed venue is well located in the heart of the action in the Kolonáki district of the city.
✉ **Tsokha 43** ☎ **729-0322**

La Joya
This very popular place features a mix of recorded music and live bands, sometimes rock as well as jazz, and also serves surprisingly good food.
✉ **Tsokha 43** ☎ **644-0030**

Stavlos
An arts complex with exhibitions and occasional movies, as well as live jazz.
✉ **Iraklidon 10** ☎ **345-2502**

Tavernas With Music

Many tavernas, mostly in the Pláka, put on late-night shows of Greek music and dancing. They are undeniably touristy, but also terrific fun. I recall frosty stares from two American matrons when the waiter picked up their table with his teeth and began dancing around with it – a Greek speciality! Shows usually begin at about 10 or 11, and generally cost a few thousand drachmae, which will include a fixed-menu meal, but not wine. Other tavernas simply offer a few Greek musicians, and a more relaxed Greek atmosphere. Some of them include:

Klimataria
You'll find more Greeks than tourists in this old favourite, featuring sing-alongs to guitar and accordion.
✉ **Klepsidras 5** ☎ **324-1809**

Taverna Mostrou
On offer here are late-night music and dancing shows, often catering to tour groups.
✉ **Mnissikleous 22** ☎ **324-2441**

Open or Closed?
As with restaurants, many music clubs close in midsummer when some of the owners and musicians go to work in the more lucrative Greek islands. Nights of opening can change too, from season to season, so ring to check before making a special journey.

Rembetika

The blues came to Greece in the 1920s when the exchange of populations with Turkey brought many displaced Greeks to slum districts such as Piraeus. Their Middle Eastern music blended with traditional Greek music to produce a mournful sound and lyrics that deal with the harsh lives of the poor and dispossessed.

Palia Taverna Kritikou
Popular with tour groups, this taverna has Cretan music and traditional dancing.
✉ Mnissikleous 24 ☎ 322-2809

Stamatopoulou Palia Plakiotiki Taverna
Locals and visitors enjoy authentic Greek music, though the only dancing is done by the customers.
✉ Lysiou 26 ☎ 322-8722

Taverna Mostrou
On offer here are late-night music and dancing shows, often catering to tour groups.
✉ Mnissikleous 22 ☎ 324-2441

Yeros tou Morea
This summer outdoor venue combines a pleasant atmosphere, good food and relaxed music.
✉ Vas. Sofias and Kokkali ☎ 728-2333

Discos/Rock Clubs

Many Athenian discos close down in the summer months and move out to the islands, where there's more action, so check listings or ring the club first. Some options include:

Ach Maria
✉ Solomou 20 ☎ 383-0086

Booze
✉ Kolokotroni 57 ☎ 324-0944

Boulevard
✉ Vouliagmenis 140, Glyfada ☎ 898-2557

The Cave
✉ Haritos 6 ☎ 722-8910

Memphis
✉ Ventiri 5 ☎ 722-4104

Mercedes Rex
✉ Panepistimiou 48 ☎ 361-4591

Rock and Roll
✉ Loukianou 6 ☎ 721-7127

Rodon
✉ Marni 24, Plateía Vathis ☎ 523-7418

Rembetika Clubs

Anifori
Out in Piraeus where *rembetika* was born, this club also features Greek folk music and is open till late.
✉ Vasileos Georgiou 47, Piraeus ☎ 411-5819
🕐 Fri–Sun

Douzeni
After a meal in one of Makriyianni's excellent eating places, move on to some late-night singing and bouzouki music.
✉ Makriyianni 8 ☎ 922-7597
🕐 Closed Sun

Ennea Ogdoa
Some rembetika nights, but otherwise Greek pop music. Great atmosphere.
✉ Alexandras 40 ☎ 823-5841/882-1095

Frankosyriani
In Exarchia, this popular venue is run by a musician.
✉ Arachovis 57 ☎ 380-0693

Rembetiki Astoria
In a neo-Classical building in Kolonáki, this appeals to a more intellectual audience.
✉ Ippokratous 181 ☎ 642-4937

Stoa Athanaton
Established favourite in the Central Market, with authentic music and good food, but book.
✉ Sofokleous 19 ☎ 321-4362
🕐 Lunch, evening. Closed Sun

Taximi
Very popular Exarchia folk/*rembetika* club.
✉ Isavron 29 ☎ 363-9919
🕐 Closed Jul–Aug

Theatre, Dance & Sport

There are many small theatrical venues in addition to the main ones such as the National Theatre. The majority of drama performances naturally are in Greek, but visitors may find an overseas company touring and performing in their own language.

Alfa
Theatre in Exarchia district.
✉ Stournara 37 ☎ 523-8742

Athinaion
Theatre near Kolonáki district.
✉ Voukourestiou 10 ☎ 323-5524

Dora Stratou Dance Theatre
This small open-air theatre at the foot of the Filopáppou Hill helps keep Greek traditional dance alive by putting on nightly performances throughout the summer tourist season. These are very popular and booking is advisable.
✉ Filopáppou ☎ 324-4395 (9–1:30; 921-4650 from 7:30PM)
🚌 Trolleybus line 9 to Filopáppou Square

Hellenic American Union Auditorium
This has a wide range of theatre and music shows, all in the English language and with, naturally, a strong American bias.
✉ Massalias 22 ☎ 362-9886

National Theatre
These are generally Greek-language productions of international dramas, though occasionally a visiting theatre group will perform in their own language. Foreign visitors might prefer one of the frequent dance or opera productions.
✉ Agiou Konstantinou 22 ☎ 523-3322

Olympia Theatre
Although home to the Greek National Opera, this theatre also puts on ballet performances.
✉ Akadimias 59 ☎ 361-2461

Pallas Theatre
A venue for major rock concerts, but it also stages some classical performances.
✉ Voukourestiou 1 ☎ 322-4434

Vrettania
Location of the central theatre near Syntagma.
✉ Panepistimiou 7 ☎ 322-1579

Sport
In addition to the options under '10 Top Activities' (▶ 71), there are also:

Football
This is an obsession in Greece, matched only by that for basketball. The local team, Panathinaikos, have their stadium (☎ 683-4000) on Leoforos Alexandras to the northeast of Lykavittós, while their rivals in Piraeus, Olympiakos, have their home at the Karaiskaki Stadium in Neo Faliro (☎ 481-2763), just short of Piraeus on the Metro.

Horse Racing
The Athens race-track is the Syngrou-Delta Faliro in Tsitsifies (☎ 941-7761), where meetings are held every Mon, Wed and Fri from 2:30 in winter and from 6PM in summer.

Dora Stratou
Dora Stratou devoted her life to preserving traditional Greek dance and music, amassing a collection of some 3,000 dance costumes in the process. Her dance troupe first performed in 1953 and, although she herself died in 1988, her memory lives on in the summer performances of Greek dance at the theatre which now bears her name.

What's on When

Movable Feasts

A number of Greek celebrations and festivities are determined by the Orthodox calendar, and could be held at different times each year. It is important, therefore, to check before travelling, especially if you wish to join in – or avoid – major festivals, especially Easter.

January

The Feast of St Basil (1 Jan): church services.
Epiphany (6 Jan): when priests bless baptismal fonts.

March

Independence Day (25 Mar): celebrates the start of the revolt against Turkish domination and features speeches and celebrations in Syntagma Square.

February/March

Carnival (*Karnaváli*) is not celebrated as widely in Greece as elsewhere in the world, though in Athens you may find impromptu music sessions in the streets, with children wearing costumes and hitting people on the head with plastic hammers. The Pláka becomes packed with Athenians.

The carnival takes place during the three weeks prior to Lent, with the biggest celebrations on the Sunday immediately before the start of Lent – seven weeks before Easter weekend.

March/April

Easter is by far the biggest and most important event in the Greek calendar, and it is well worth visiting Athens and other parts of Greece to witness the festivities. Churches will be open prior to Easter weekend as people prepare for the festivities. The bier on which Christ's body will be laid is decorated with flowers, and on Friday evening is carried through the streets. On Easter Saturday evening the main church service takes place, climaxing at midnight. On Easter Sunday families get together for big celebrations.

May

Labour Day (1 May): in common with many other countries, there are traditional workers' parades.

May/Jun

Whit (Feast of the Holy Spirit): seven weeks (50 days) after the Greek Easter, Whit Sunday and Monday are also celebrated. Monday is a national holiday with parades and parties.

Summer

Summer brings the annual Athens Festival. A special box office for tickets to events opens in the early summer in the arcade at Stadiou 4 ☎ 322-1459. Mon–Sat 8:30–2, 5–7, Sun 10:30–1.

In July and August is the *Daphni Wine Festival*.

August

Feast of the Assumption (15 Aug): when Greeks make an effort to return to their home villages, and ferries are often full. This is therefore a bad time to be travelling to or from Athens.

October

Óchi Day (28 Oct): in honour of the Greek leader, General Metaxas, who allegedly gave a one-word response of 'Óchi' (No) to Mussolini's request that his troops be allowed to pass through Greece. Syntagma is the focal point, but parades are held throughout the city.

December

The Greek year winds down with *Christmas* and *New Year's Eve*, though these are not as important to the Greeks as Easter.

Practical Matters

Above: postcards on sale in
abundance
Right: no chance of getting
lost in the city

TIME DIFFERENCES

GMT	Athens	Germany	USA (NY)	Netherlands	Spain
12 noon	→ 2PM	→ 1PM	← 7AM	→ 1PM	→ 1PM

BEFORE YOU GO

WHAT YOU NEED

- ● Required
- ○ Suggested
- ▲ Not required

	UK	Germany	USA	Netherlands	Spain
Passport/National Identity Card	●	●	●	●	●
Visa	▲	▲	▲	▲	▲
Onward or Return Ticket	▲	▲	▲	▲	▲
Health Inoculations	○	○	○	○	○
Health Documentation (Reciprocal Agreements ➤ 123, Health)	●	●	▲	●	●
Travel Insurance	●	●	●	●	●
Driving Licence (National or International)	●	●	●	●	●
Car Insurance Certificate (if own car)	●	●	●	●	●
Car Registration Document (if own car)	●	●	●	●	●

WHEN TO GO

Athens

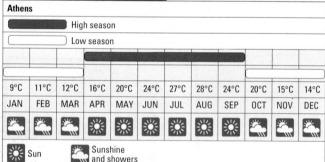

High season

Low season

9°C	11°C	12°C	16°C	20°C	24°C	27°C	28°C	24°C	20°C	15°C	14°C
JAN	FEB	MAR	APR	MAY	JUN	JUL	AUG	SEP	OCT	NOV	DEC

Sun

Sunshine and showers

TOURIST OFFICES

In the UK
National Tourist
Organisation of Greece
(NTOG)
4 Conduit Street
London W1R 0DJ
☎ 0171 734 5997
Fax: 0171 287 1369

In the USA
National Tourist
Organisation of Greece
645 Fifth Avenue
New York
NY 10022
☎ 212/421 5777
Fax: 212/826 6940

611 West Sixth Street
Suite 2198
Los Angeles
CA 92668
☎ 213/626 6696
Fax: 213/489 9744

POLICE 100

FIRE 199

AMBULANCE 166

TOURIST POLICE 171 (Athens) 902-5992 (outside Athens)

WHEN YOU ARE THERE

ARRIVING

Greece's national airline, Olympic Airways, has scheduled flights to the West terminal at Athens's Ellinikon International Airport from major cities around the world. All other airlines use the East Terminal, a five-minute drive away. Charter flights are much cheaper in season.

Ellinikón International Airport, Athens Kilometres to city centre	Journey Times
	🚃 N/A
10 kilometres	🚌 30 minutes
	🚗 25 minutes

Thessaloniki Airport Kilometres to city centre	Journey times
	🚃 25 minutes
10 kilometres	🚌 60 minutes
	🚗 15 minutes

MONEY

Greece's currency is the drachma (dr), issued in notes of 100, 200, 500, 1,000, 5,000 and 10,000 drachma, and coins of 5, 10, 20, 50 and 100 drachma. Travellers' cheques are accepted by most hotels, shops and restaurants, although the rate of exchange may be less favourable than in banks. Travellers' cheques in sterling or US dollars are the most convenient. There are banks on almost every street in Athens, and money exchange offices, where travellers' cheques, cash and Eurocheques can be exchanged and advances on credit cards obtained.

TIME

🕐 Athens is two hours ahead of Greenwich Mean Time (GMT+2), but is three hours ahead from the end of March, when clocks go forward one hour, until late October.

CUSTOMS

 YES

Goods obtained Duty Free inside the EU or goods bought outside the EU (Limits):
Alcohol (over 22% vol): 1L *or* Alcohol (not over 22% vol): 2L *and*
Still table wine: 2L,
Cigarettes: 200 *or* Cigars: 50 *or* Tobacco: 250gms
Perfume: 60ml
Toilet water: 250ml
Goods bought Duty and Tax Paid for own use inside the EU (Guidance Levels):
Alcohol (over 22% vol): 10L
Alcohol (not over 22% vol): 20L *and* Wine (max 60L sparkling): 90L Beer: 110L
Cigarettes: 800, Cigars: 200, Tobacco: 1kg
Perfume and Toilet Water: no limit
You must be 17 or over to benefit from alcohol and tobacco allowances.

 NO

Drugs, firearms, ammunition, offensive weapons (includes flick knives), obscene material, unlicensed animals.

EMBASSIES AND CONSULATES

UK	Germany	USA	Netherlands	Spain
723 6211	728 5111	721 2951	723 9701	721 4885

WHEN YOU ARE THERE

TOURIST OFFICES

Greek National Tourist Office
Amerikis 2
☎ 331 0561

The above is the administrative office and also now has a new information office open from 11–1 Mon–Fri, but this should increase. The Athens Municipality also has an information booth on the corner of Syntagma and Ermou. There is an information desk at the airport's East Terminal (969 4500) and at Marina Zeas in Piraeus (428 4100). In summer the GNTO opens an office at Stadiou 4 (322 1459) for dealing with the Athens Festival.

NATIONAL HOLIDAYS

J	F	M	A	M	J	J	A	S	O	N	D
2	(2)	1(3)	(1)	1(1)	1		1		1		2

1 Jan	New Year's Day
6 Jan	Epiphany
Feb/Mar	Greek 'Carnival' season, three weeks before the beginning of Lent.
Feb/Mar	Shrove Monday (41 days pre-Easter)
25 Mar	Independence Day
Mar/Apr	Good Friday, Easter Monday
1 May	Labour Day
May/Jun	Whit Monday (50 days after Easter)
15 Aug	Feast of the Assumption of the Blessed Virgin Mary
28 Oct	Óchi Day
25/26 Dec	Christmas

Restaurants and tourist shops may well stay open on these days, but museums will be closed.

OPENING HOURS

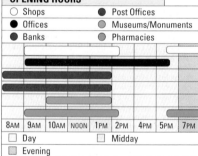

○ Shops   ● Post Offices
● Offices   ◐ Museums/Monuments
● Banks   ◐ Pharmacies

| 8AM | 9AM | 10AM | NOON | 1PM | 2PM | 4PM | 5PM | 7PM |

☐ Day   ☐ Midday
☐ Evening

Pharmacies normally open on weekdays only. Monasteries open during daylight hours; churches are often open all day, though some may open early morning and evenings only. Opening hours are flexible, especially those of museums, which change annually, if only by 15 minutes or so. Longer hours operate in summer, so check if travelling between October and Easter. Four post offices open late: Metropoleos, Syntagma; Aïolou 100, Omonia Square; Metropoleos Square; East Terminal, Athens Airport. Mon–Fri until 8; Sat, Sun mornings (not Metropoleos).

DRIVE ON THE
RIGHT

TOILETS
FREE

PUBLIC TRANSPORT

Internal Flights Domestic flights are operated by Olympic Airways, and it is possible to make connections at Athens and Thessaloníki to several provincial airports, and to the Greek Islands. Domestic tickets on Olympic Airways are non-transferable, and a no-smoking policy is operated on all their internal flights.

Trains There are two railway stations in Athens, Peloponnisou (☎ 513 1601) for the Peloponnese and nearby Larissis (☎ 823 7741) for lines north. Services are more restricted than in other countries, due partly to the terrain and partly to the well-established excellent bus service. For timetable information ☎ 145/6/7.

Metro One metro line runs from Kifisia in the north to Piraeus in the south, though not all trains run the full length. Journeys are cheap, based on a zone system. Another line running roughly east–west is under construction, but a long way from completion. Trains run every five minutes from 5AM to 12:15AM.

Buses Despite a huge network, this is not the best way to get around Athens. Tickets (100 dr), are valid for one journey and must be bought in advance from a booth near the bus stop, or certain kiosks and shops. They must then be punched on the machine on board, though buses can be so crowded it is impossible to reach the machine.

Ferries/Hydrofoils The main ferry port in Athens is Piraeus which runs services to mainland towns and certain islands. There are several different harbours here, some distance apart, so be sure to check from which harbour your service departs. Timetables can be obtained from offices of NTOG.

CAR RENTAL

Most leading car rental companies have offices in Athens, many along Syngrou. Most also have desks at the airport terminals. Car hire is expensive, and accident rates are high. The minimum age for car rental ranges from 21 to 25.

TAXIS

Beware the rogue driver with a broken meter. Drivers may stop to pick up other passengers en route. Half the private cars are banned from central Athens on any one day, so book a taxi ahead if the journey is important. Otherwise, hail a cab.

DRIVING

Speed limit on motorways: 120kph

Speed limit outside built-up areas: 80kph

Speed limit in built-up areas: 50kph

Seat belts must be worn in front seats at all times and in rear seats where fitted. Children under 10 are not allowed in front seats.

80 micrograms of alcohol in 100ml of breath is a criminal offence, and from 50–80 micrograms a civil offence. Penalties are severe.

Petrol (*venzíni*) usually comes in five grades: super (*sooper*), regular (*aplí*), unleaded (*amolyvdhi*), super unleaded (*sooper amolyvdhi*) and diesel (*petrelaio*). Petrol stations are normally open 7–7 (closed Sun) though larger ones open 24 hours. Most take credit cards. There are few stations in remote areas.

If you break down driving your own car then the Automobile and Touring Club of Greece (ELPA) (☎ 779-1615) provide 24-hour road assistance (☎ 104). If the car is hired, follow the instructions given in the documentation; most of the international rental firms provide a rescue service.

PERSONAL SAFETY

Greece is one of the safest countries in the world and you are unlikely to experience any problems. Nevertheless, Athens is a city like any other, with impoverished migrants and drug addicts desperate for cash, so exercise the usual precautions.

● Beware of pickpockets in markets, tourist sights or crowded places.
● Avoid walking alone in unlit streets at night.

Tourist Police:
☎ **171**
from any call box

TELEPHONES

Most public telephones now accept only phonecards, available from kiosks and some shops in units of 100. Otherwise, use the phone available at most roadside kiosks: your call is metred and you pay in cash. Some hotels, restaurants and bars have phones accepting 10, 20, 50 and 100 dr coins. For the operator dial 132 or 131.

International Dialling Codes

From Athens to:	
UK:	00 44
Germany:	00 49
USA & Canada:	00 1
Netherlands:	00 31
Spain:	00 34

POST

POST

Post Offices (*takhydhromio*) are distinguished by a yellow OTE sign, and many cash travellers' cheques and exchange currency. They are normally open morning shop hours only, except for a couple of main branches (► 120). Queues can be long so if you only want stamps, (*ghramatósima*), try kiosks or shops selling postcards.

ELECTRICITY

The power supply in Athens is 220 volts AC, 50 Hz.

 Sockets accept two-pin round plugs, so an adaptor is needed for most non-Continental European appliances and a transformer for appliances operating on other voltages.

TIPS/GRATUITIES

Yes ✓ No ✗		
Restaurants (service not inc.)	✓	10–15%
Cafés/bars (service not inc.)	✓	change
Tour guides	✓	500 drachma
Hairdressers	✓	change
Taxis	✓	change
Chambermaids	✓	100 dr per day
Porters	✓	500 drachma
Cloakroom attendants	✓	change
Toilets	✓	change

What to photograph: The classic sights, markets, Byzantine churches.
When to photograph: Early morning is best both for the light and avoiding the crowds. Photograph again when the sun starts to go down. In dark and narrow streets, such as in the flea market, you may want to shoot when the sun is high in the sky.
Where to buy film: Film is readily available from tourist shops and camera shops throughout the city.

HEALTH

Insurance
Visitors from European Union (EU) countries are entitled to reciprocal state medical care in Athens with form E111, available from post offices. This only covers treatment in the most basic of hospitals, and private medical insurance is still advised and is essential for all other visitors.

Dental Services
Free treatment is available at the Piraeus Dentistry School and the Evanghelismios Hospital. See the telephone directory for private dentists or ask at your hotel or embassy. Treatment should be covered by private medical insurance.

Sun Advice
The sunniest months are July and August with daytime temperatures well up into the 30s and sometimes over 40°C. Avoid the midday sun and use a strong sunblock. Don't underestimate the dehydration effects of walking around sightseeing – drink lots of water.

Drugs
Prescription and non-prescription drugs and medicines are available from pharmacies (*farmakia*), distinguished by a large green cross. Note that codeine is banned in Greece and you can be fined for carrying it.

Safe Water
Tap water is perfectly safe, but bottled water is widely available.

CONCESSIONS

Students/Youth Holders of an International Student Identity Card (ISIC) are eligible for concessions on travel, museum entrance fees etc. There is no YMCA but there is a women-only hostel, XEN (YWCA) at Amerikis 11. Try also the Athens Connection hostel at Ioulianou 20 (☎ 822-4592).

Senior Citizens Most museums and archaeological sites have reduced rates for elderly visitors. There are few other concessions, but senior citizens can take advantage of off-season rates. Concessions are available on travel and entrance fees. Always carry your passport for proof of age.

THE GREEK ALPHABET

The Greek alphabet cannot be transliterated into other languages in a straight-forward way. This can lead to variations in romanised spellings of Greek words and placenames. It also leads inevitably to inconsistencies, especially when comparing different guide books, leaflets and signs. However, the differences rarely make any name unrecognisable. The language looks complex, but it is worth memorising the alphabet to help with signs, destinations etc.

Alpha	Αα	short a, as in hat
Beta	Ββ	v sound
Gamma	Γγ	guttural g sound
Delta	Δδ	hard th, as in father
Epsilon	Εε	short e
Zita	Ζζ	z sound
Eta	Ηη	long e, as in feet
Theta	Θθ	soft th, as in think
Iota	Ιι	short i, as in hit
Kappa	Κκ	k sound
Lambda	Λλ	l sound
Mu	Μμ	m sound
Nu	Νν	n sound
Xi	Ξξ	x or ks sound
Omicron	Οο	short o, as in pot
Pi	Ππ	p sound
Rho	Ρρ	r sound
Sigma	Σσ	s sound
Tau	Ττ	t sound
Upsilon	Υυ	ee, or y as in funny
Phi	Φφ	f sound
Chi	Χχ	guttural ch, as in loch
Psi	Ψψ	ps, as in chops
Omega	Ωω	long o, as in bone

WHEN DEPARTING

- Remember to confirm your flight details at least three days before departure, and leave a contact number with the airline in case of late changes.
- Remember which air terminal you need (West for Olympic, otherwise East).
- Allow plenty of time to negotiate the Athenian traffic.

LANGUAGE

For the Greek alphabet (➤ 123). The Greek language can look daunting to the visitor, and certainly sounds it because the Greeks speak with a machine-gun rapidity. Although transliterations vary, learning the alphabet will help with road signs and bus destinations, as romanisations will vary, but not a great deal. It is also worth trying to learn a few basic courtesy phrases; the Greeks themselves know how difficult their language is and appreciate the visitor's attempts to learn it.

hotel	xenothokhio	room service	servis thomatiou
bed and breakfast	thomatio meh proino	chambermaid	kamaryera
		bath	banyera
single room	monoklino	shower	doos
double room	diklino	toilet	tooaleta
one person	ena atomo	balcony	balkoni
one night	mia nikhta	key	klithi
reservation	mia kratisi	sea view	vthea ti thalasa

bank	trapeza	credit card	pistotiki karta
exchange office	sarafiko	exchange rate	sinalagmatiki
post office	takhithromio	commission	isotimia
coin	kerma	charge	parangelia
banknote	khartonomisma	cashier	tamias
cheque	epitayi	change	resta
travellers' cheque	taxithiotiki epitayi	foreign currency	khartonomismes xenes

café	café	starter	proto piato
pub/bar	bar	main course	kirio piato
breakfast	proino	dessert	glikisma
lunch	yevma	bill	logariasmos
dinner	mesimeriano	beer	bira
table	trapezi	wine	krasi
waiter	garson	water	nero
waitress	garsona	coffee	café

airport	aerothromio	single ticket	apio
train	treno	return ticket	isitirio met epistrofis
bus	leoforio		
station	stathmos	non-smoking	khoros ya mi kapnizondes
boat	plio		
port	limani	car	aftokinito
ticket	isitirio	petrol	venzini
ferry	feribot	bus stop	stasi leoforiou

yes	neh	excuse me	signomi
no	ochi	you're welcome	parakalo
please	parakalo	how are you?	pos iseh?
thank you	efharisto	do you speak English?	milate Anglika?
hello	ya sas		
goodbye	adio	I don't under- stand	dhen katalaveno
good morning	kali mera		
good evening	kali spera	how much?	poso?
goodnight	kali nichta	open	aniktos
where is...?	pou einai...?	closed	klistos

INDEX

INDEX

Acknowledgements

The Automobile Association wishes to thank the following photographers and libraries for their assistance in the preparation of this book:

MARY EVANS PICTURE LIBRARY 10b, 14c; ROBERT HARDING PICTURE LIBRARY 85b; HULTON GETTY 11b; MIKE GERRARD 6b, 22b, 27b, 32, 36b, 37a, 52b, 53c, 56b, 65b, 67, 91b, 117a, 117b; NATURE PHOTOGRAPHERS LTD 12b; REX FEATURES 14b; SPECTRUM COLOUR LIBRARY 62a, 84; WORLD PICTURES F/cover c (man in costume), 13b, 64, 71b.

The remaining photographs are held in the Association's own photo library (AA PHOTO LIBRARY) and were taken by Richard Surman with the exception of the following: TERRY HARRIS F/cover b (Parthenon), B/cover (tomatoes), 1, 8c, 25b, 33b, 34, 36a, 37b, 38, 46b, 50a, 50b, 61b, 72, 77b, 80/1; JAMES TIMS 87; PETER WILSON F/cover d (worry beads), 2, 5a, 5b, 6a, 7a, 7b, 8a, 8b, 9a, 9b, 9c, 10a, 11a, 12a, 12c, 13a, 14a, 16b, 17b, 18b, 19b, 18/19, 20b, 20c, 21a, 21b, 23, 24, 26b, 31b, 35b, 40b, 42b. 44b. 45b. 47b, 51b,53b, 54, 55, 58b, 59b, 60b, 60c, 61a, 63, 66b, 69b, 74/5, 86, 89b, 90, 91a.

Author's Acknowledgements

The author would like to thank Panos Argyros and Claire Carroll of the the National Tourist Association of Greece in London, and Kostas Zissis of the Attalos Hotel in Athens.

Copy editor: Sally MacEachern